Amazing Facts about Australia

Text by Pat Slater

Steve Parish
DISCOVER & LEARN
ABOUT AUSTRALIA

www.steveparish.com.au

Contents

About Australia today

Sydney, capital of the State of New South Wales, seen across Sydney Harbour.

The city centre of Melbourne, capital of the State of Victoria, viewed across the city's War Memorial and down St Kilda Road.

Landmarks of Canberra, Australia's national capital, with Old Parliament House in front of the present Parliament House.

Australia is an island continent, whose landscapes, plants and animals have developed in unique ways since it was cut off from other landmasses. Over the past 50 000 years, it has undergone repeated climate changes – the present ᴳEl Niño/ᴳLa Niña cycle, which brings alternating droughts and floods to much of the continent, is only the latest of these.

People have lived in Australia for a very long time. The Aboriginal people had their own ways of managing the country they lived in. Non-ᴳindigenous people arrived more than 200 years ago, and their ways of life changed the country's landscapes and living things in sudden and drastic ways. Today's Australia has been shaped by the interaction between humans and the land and its plants and animals.

This book takes the reader on a journey around Australia's States and Territories, exploring their major cities and regions. Its facts and pictures tell a wealth of fascinating stories about this great country and the living things to which it is home.

Adelaide, capital of South Australia, seen across the parklands of North Adelaide and the River Torrens.

Perth, capital of Western Australia. In the foreground are the Swan River, Mill Point and the Narrows Bridge. Centre left is Kings Park, centre right is Perth Water.

A view of Hobart, capital of Tasmania, showing Battery Point, Sandy Bay and the estuary of the Derwent River.

About this book

This book is an introduction to our magnificent land, which will, we hope, inspire readers to make their own investigations and discoveries. Further information can be found in books and from videos, CD-ROMs and the Internet. Explore your local district first, then plan further journeys to make when you are able to do so.

Words marked with a ^{G} in the text can be found explained and enlarged upon in the Glossary on page 79. National Park is abbreviated to NP.

Some of the references we used in finding out about Australia as well as suggestions for further reading are listed on the inside back cover, and your local library will probably contain many other interesting books, CDs, films and other materials.

Brisbane, capital of the State of Queensland, seen across the lower reaches of the Brisbane River.

Darwin, capital of the Northern Territory, viewed over Port Darwin and Darwin Harbour.

How old is it?

Captain Cook's parents' cottage, now in Melbourne, was built in the 1750s.

Cadman's Cottage in The Rocks, Sydney was built in 1816.

Parliament House, Canberra, was opened in 1988.

Pollen from the ancestors of these Antarctic Beech trees has been dated to more than 66 million years before the present.

Some Aboriginal rock engravings, or petroglyphs, were chipped into rock over 40 000 years ago.

Aboriginal people have been painting on the walls of caves in Kakadu NP for more than 50 000 years.

Stromatolites at Shark Bay, WA, represent forms of life which first appeared over 3500 million years ago.

Crocodile-like reptiles lived in Australia over 110 million years ago. Saltwater Crocodiles (above) have survived in Australia since dinosaurs roamed the Earth more than 65 million years ago.

Waterlilies were growing in Australia more than 100 million years ago.

The sandstones of the Kennedy Range in WA were laid down under the sea more than 250 million years ago. Earth movements brought them to the surface and they have been weathered into the range we see today.

Geikie Gorge, in the Kimberley of WA, is part of a limestone coral reef which grew in warm coastal waters in the Devonian era more than 350 million years ago.

A human timeline for Australia

2000	Olympic Games held in Sydney, NSW.
1994	Existence of Wollemi pine disclosed.
1993	Sydney announced host city of Olympics.
1988	Bicentenary of European settlement.
	Parliament House, Canberra, opened.
1983	Lower Gordon-Franklin dam stopped.
1982	TV story reveals Purnululu to the world.
1981	Sydney Tower opened.
	Great Barrier Reef World Heritage-listed.
1975	Tasman Bridge, Hobart, collapses.
1974	Australian Institute of Sport founded.
	Cyclone Tracy destroys Darwin.
1973	Completion of Snowy Mountains Scheme.
	Sydney Opera House opened.
1972	Lake Pedder, Tas., flooded.
1971	First Green Ban protects Heritage area.
1964	World land speed record set on Lake Eyre.
1963	Lake Burley Griffin, Canberra, filled.
1959	Construction Sydney Opera House begins.
1956	Olympic Games held in Melbourne.
1950s	British atomic tests at Maralinga, SA.
1949	Snowy Mountains Scheme begins.
1945	End of World War II.
1942	Darwin bombed.
1941	Australian War Memorial, Canberra, opened.
1939	Australia enters World War II.
1936	Thylacine declared protected.
1932	Sydney Harbour Bridge opened.
	Great Ocean Road completed.
1924	Mt Isa Mines formed.
1919	Great Ocean Road begun.
1918	End of World War I.
1915	Landing of ANZ troops at Gallipoli.
1914	Australia enters World War I.
1913	Construction of Canberra begins.
1911	Site for Canberra acquired.
1910	Flinders St Station, Melbourne, completed.
1908	Canberra to be Australia's capital.
1905	Wilsons Promontory, Vic, made a national park.
1901	Federation creates Commonwealth of Australia.
1898	Hampden Bridge, Kangaroo Valley, opened.
1894	Women given the vote SA.
1892	Gold discovered at Coolgardie, WA.
1881	First census — 2.25 million Europeans.
1880	Ned Kelly hanged in Melbourne,Vic.
1878	First Stawell Gift foot race run, Stawell, Vic.
1877	Australia wins first cricket Test v. England.
1871	Australia linked to world by telegraph.
1869	Settlement at Darwin, NT.
1868	Transportation of convicts to WA stops.
1862	First Melbourne Cup.
1861	Eureka Stockade rebellion at Ballarat.

1854	Transportation to Tasmania stops.
1853	Melbourne Zoo opened.
1851	Gold discovered in NSW and Vic.
1850	Convicts arrive in WA.
1842	Moreton Bay a free settlement.
1840	Transportation of convicts to NSW ends.
	Mt Kosciuszko climbed by Strzelecki.
1836	Settlement at Glenelg, Adelaide, SA.
1835	European settlement on Yarra River, Vic.
1830s	New England Tableland, NSW, settled.
	James Busby plants vines in Hunter Valley.
1830	Penal settlement at Port Arthur, Tas.
1829	Settlement on Swan River (Perth), WA.
1825	Van Diemen's Land (Tas.) a separate colony.
1824–25	Convict settlement at Moreton Bay, Qld.
1823	Richmond Bridge, Tasmania, completed.
1813	Blue Mts crossed, opening lands beyond.
1805	Settlement at Launceston, Tas.
1803–04	Settlement at Hobart, Tas.
1788	First Fleet arrives at Botany Bay, NSW.
1770	Cook (*Endeavour*) sails up east coast.
1712	Zuytdorp wrecked on WA coast.
1696–97	Willem de Vlamingh sails coast of WA.
1642–44	Abel Tasman circumnavigates Aust.
1629	*Batavia* wrecked on Houtman Abrolhos.
1623	*Arnhem* explores northern coast of NT.
1622	*Leeuwin* sights corner of WA.
1616	Dirk Hartog (*Eendracht*) at Shark Bay, WA.
1606	Luis de Torres sails through Torres Strait.
	Willem Jansz (*Duyfken*) lands on Cape York.
1500s	Macassans begin voyages to NT.
1200s	Aborigines in Vic. build stone huts.
AD	Anno Domini (in the year of Our Lord)
0	Birth of Christ
b.p.	before the present
4000	Dingo arrives in Australia.
12 000	Sea covers land bridge to Tasmania.
13 000	Ice Age ends.
18 000	Height of Ice Age. Humans living in Tas.
20 000	Bradshaw rock art painted in Kimberley.
	Final survivors of ᴳmegafauna disappear.
30 000	Funeral ceremony used at Lake Mungo.
32 000	Engravings on stone Cape York Peninsula.
35 000	Humans living in Warreen Cave, Tas.
37 000	Humans living at Mount Mulligan, Qld.
38 000	Humans living on Upper Swan River, WA.
40 000	Humans living at Lake Mungo, NSW.
44 000	Engravings on stone at Olary, SA.
50 000	Rock art in Arnhem Land, NT.
60 000+	Humans first appear in Australia.

Australia political

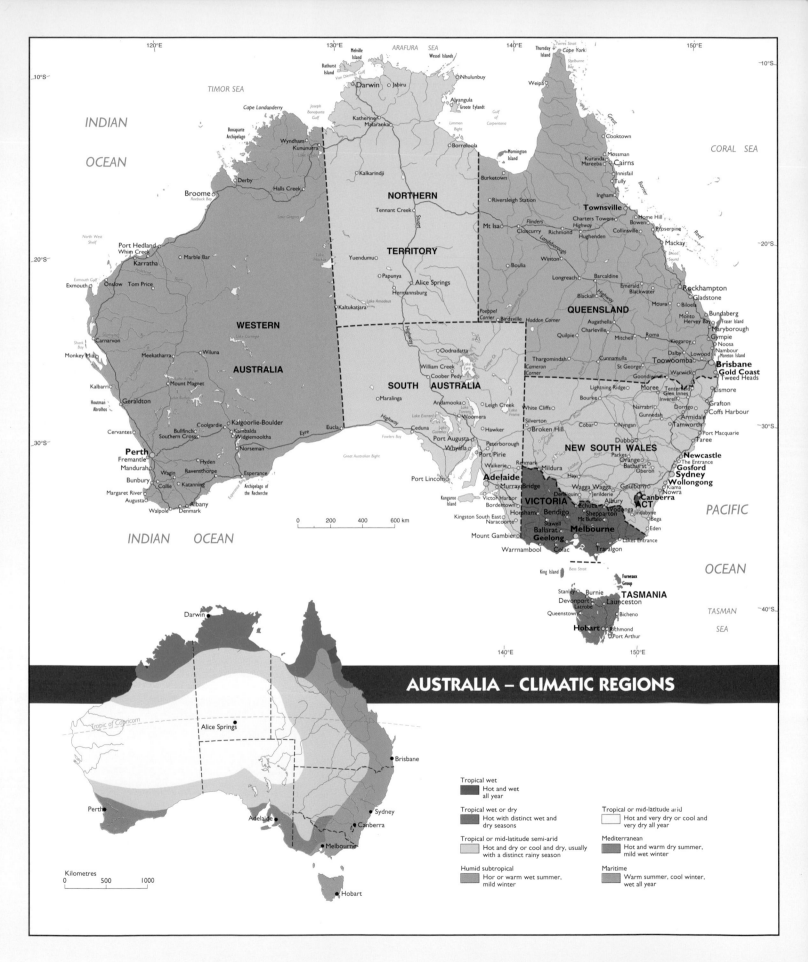

AUSTRALIA – CLIMATIC REGIONS

Tropical wet
Hot and wet all year

Tropical wet or dry
Hot with distinct wet and dry seasons

Tropical or mid-latitude semi-arid
Hot and dry or cool and dry, usually with a distinct rainy season

Humid subtropical
Hot or warm wet summer, mild winter

Tropical or mid-latitude arid
Hot and very dry or cool and very dry all year

Mediterranean
Hot and warm dry summer, mild wet winter

Maritime
Warm summer, cool winter, wet all year

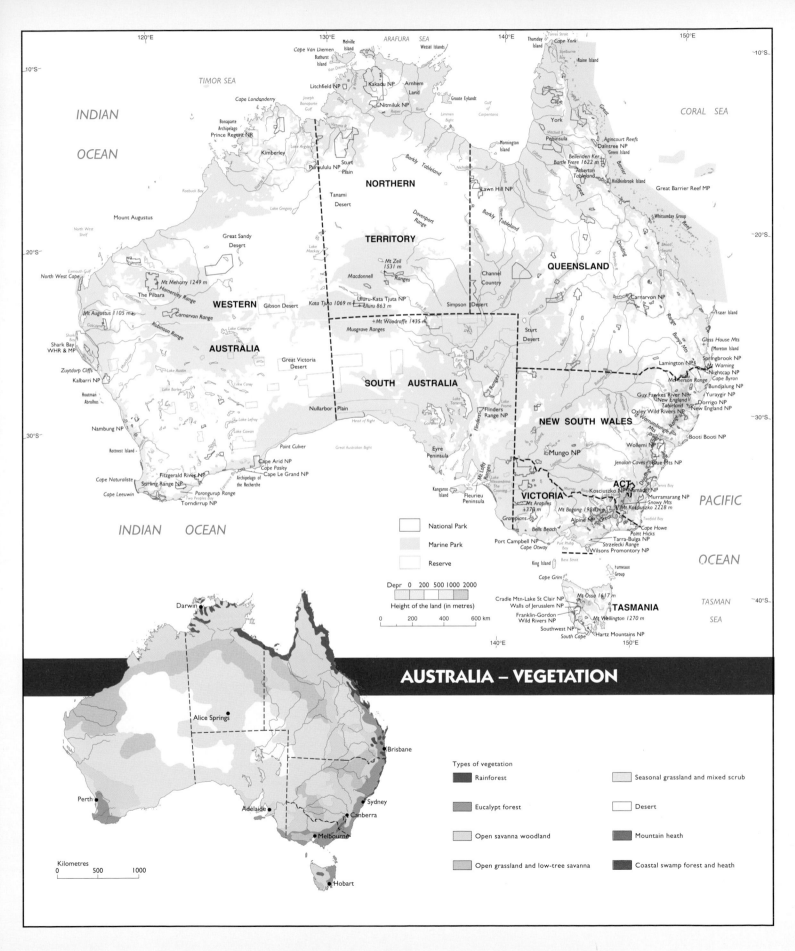

INDIAN OCEAN

TIMOR SEA

ARAFURA SEA

CORAL SEA

Cape Van Diemen
Melville Island
Bathurst Island
Van Diemen Gulf
Cape Londonderry
Joseph Bonaparte Gulf
Litchfield NP
Kakadu NP
Arnhem Land
Wessel Islands
Cape York
Thursday Island
Torres Strait
Sjoburne
Raine Island

Bonaparte Archipelago
Prince Regent NR
Kimberley
Lake Argyle
Sturt Plain
Nitmiluk NP
Roper River
Groote Eylandt
Gulf of Carpentaria
Limmen Bight
Cape York Peninsula
Agincourt Reefs
Daintree NP
Green Island
Bellenden Ker
Bartle Frere 1622 m
Atherton Tableland
Hinchinbrook Island
Great Barrier Reef MP

Roebuck Bay
Purnululu NP
NORTHERN
Tanami Desert
Barkly Tableland
Nicholson R.
Lawn Hill NP
Barkly Tableland

North West Shelf
Great Sandy Desert
TERRITORY
Davenport Range
Mitchell R.
Whitsunday Group
Broad Sound

North West Cape
Exmouth Gulf
Mt Meharry 1249 m
Hamersley Range
The Pilbara
Lake Gregory
Lake Mackay
Mt Zeil 1531 m
Macdonnell Ranges
QUEENSLAND
Carnarvon NP

Mount Augustus
WESTERN
Gibson Desert
Kata Tjuta 1069 m
Uluru-Kata Tjuta NP
Uluru 863 m
Channel Country
Simpson Desert
Fraser Island

Mt Augustus 1105 m
Carnarvon Range
Robinson Range
Lake Carnegie
+Mt Woodroffe 1435 m
Musgrave Ranges
Sturt Desert
Cooper Ck
Bunya Mts
Glass House Mts
+Moreton Island

Shark Bay
Shark Bay WHR & MP
AUSTRALIA
Lake Austin
Lake Barlee
Great Victoria Desert
SOUTH AUSTRALIA
Lamington NP
Mt Warning
Nightcap NP
Cape Byron
Macpherson Range
Bundjalung NP

Zuytdorp Cliffs
Kalbarri NP
Houtman Abrolhos
Lake Lefroy
Lake Cowan
Nullarbor Plain
Flinders Range NP
NEW SOUTH WALES
Guy Fawkes River NP
New England Tableland
Oxley Wild Rivers NP
Yuraygir NP
Dorrigo NP
New England NP

Nambung NP
Point Culver
Great Australian Bight
Head of Bight
Lake Torrens
Lake Frome
Lake Eyre
Lake Gairdner
Warrumbungle Mts
Wollemi NP
Booti Booti NP

Rottnest Island
Eyre Peninsula
Mungo NP
Jenolan Caves
Blue Mts NP

Perth
Cape Arid NP
Cape Pasley
Cape Le Grand NP
Archipelago of the Recherche
Kangaroo Island
Fleurieu Peninsula
Lake Alexandrina
The Coorong
Mt Lofty Ranges
ACT
Kosciuszko NP
Namadgi NP
Murramarang NP
Snowy Mts
PACIFIC

Narrabeen NP
Fitzgerald River NP
Stirling Range NP
Porongurup Range
Two Peoples Bay
Torndirrup NP
VICTORIA
Mt Arapiles +370 m
Mt Bogong 1986 m
+Mt Kosciuszko 2228 m
Alpine NP
Cape Howe
Point Hicks

Cape Naturaliste
Cape Leeuwin
Grampians
Bells Beach
Port Campbell NP
Cape Otway
Port Phillip Bay
Tarra-Bulga NP
Strzelecki Range
Wilsons Promontory NP
OCEAN

King Island
Bass Strait
Cape Grim
Furneaux Group
TASMAN SEA

Cradle Mtn-Lake St Clair NP
Walls of Jerusalem NP
Mt Ossa 1617 m
TASMANIA
Franklin-Gordon Wild Rivers NP
Mt Wellington 1270 m
Southwest NP
South Cape
Hartz Mountains NP

National Park

Marine Park

Reserve

Depr 0 200 500 1000 2000
Height of the land (in metres)

0 200 400 600 km

AUSTRALIA – VEGETATION

Darwin

Alice Springs

Brisbane

Perth

Adelaide

Sydney
Canberra

Melbourne

Hobart

Kilometres
0 500 1000

Types of vegetation

Rainforest

Eucalypt forest

Open savanna woodland

Open grassland and low-tree savanna

Seasonal grassland and mixed scrub

Desert

Mountain heath

Coastal swamp forest and heath

NEW SOUTH WALES

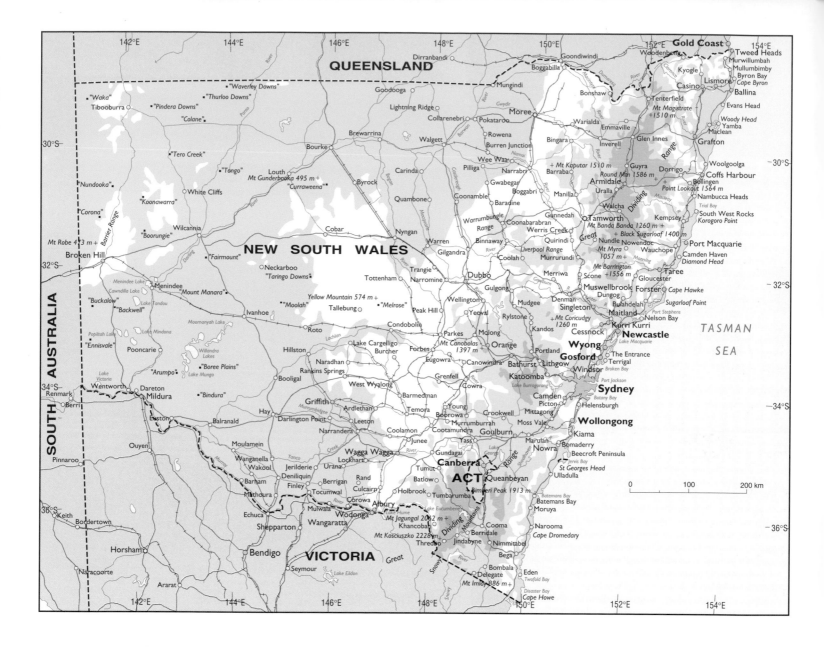

FACTS FACTS FACTS FACTS FACTS FACTS FACTS FACTS FACTS FACTS FACTS FACTS FACTS FACTS

▶ NSW is home to more than 80 440 indigenous people, about 26.5% of Australia's total.

▶ NSW was a dumping ground for British convicts from 1788 to 1840. Some Australians have convict forebears.

▶ Sydney, NSW, is home to people of 140 cultures, who speak more than 80 languages.

▶ Inland NSW is drained by Australia's longest river system, the Murray (2530 km)–Darling (1900 km).

▶ NSW produces ⅔ of Australia's black coal, most of its wheat and has over ⅓ of its sheep.

▶ Record NSW rainfalls: 136 mm in 1 hour, Wongawilly, 18.2.1984; 809 mm in 24 hours, Dorrigo, 21.2.1954.

▶ Jenolan (300 caves) is NSW's biggest cave system. The deepest mainland caves are at Yarrangobilly, in Kosciuszko NP, NSW.

▶ Ball's Pyramid, 30 km S of Lord Howe I, is part of NSW. At 561 m high it is the world's highest rock.

▶ In September, 1993, Sydney, capital of NSW was announced as host city of the year 2000 Olympic Games. Homebush Bay is the site of Olympic Park and the athletes' village. The main stadium has a capacity of 110 000.

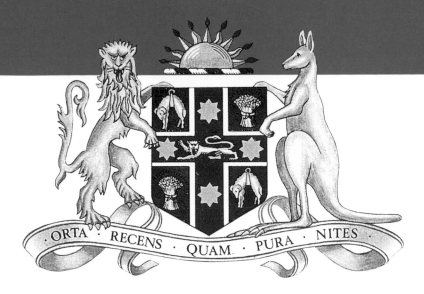

THE PREMIER STATE

Founded in 1788, New South Wales is Australia's oldest State. It is bordered by Queensland, Victoria, South Australia and the Pacific Ocean. Running the length of the east coast is a narrow coastal plain. To its west is the Great Dividing Range. Beyond the mountains, a tableland gradually slopes down to plains which cover most of the State.

NSW has more than six million people, most of whom live along the coast. More than half the population lives in the capital, Sydney.

The NSW Coat of Arms has the British lion and the Australian kangaroo holding up a shield. On this is the red cross of St George on which are four stars depicting the Southern Cross, and the British lion. Two ᴳquarterings of the shield show the Golden Fleece and two show wheat sheaves. The crest is a rising sun, representative of a newly rising country.

SYDNEY (central coast)				
	Jan	Apr	Jul	Oct
max °C	26	22	16	22
min °C	19	15	8	13
rainfall mm	104	126	101	79
rainy days	12	12	10	12

THREDBO (alpine region)				
	Jan	Apr	Jul	Oct
max °C	21	14	5	13
min °C	7	2	-4	2
rainfall mm	110	131	144	220
rainy days	11	13	16	17

The flag of New South Wales.

The motto, Orta recens quam pura nites, means "Newly risen, how brightly you shine", referring to the State's continuing progress and development.

KNOW MORE ABOUT NEW SOUTH WALES

Total area: 801 600 km² (10.43% Australian total)
Coastline length: 1900 km
Population: 6 116 200

Highest point: Mt Kosciuszko (2228 m)
Furthest point east: Cape Byron (153°38'E)

Coldest place: Charlotte Pass (-23.0°C on 28.6.1994)
Most snow in one year: Charlotte Pass (7.9 m in 1947)

Hottest place: Bourke (52.8°C on 17.1.1877)
ᴳ**Emblems:** Waratah, Platypus and Laughing Kookaburra

NSW coastline at Crowdy Bay.

Byron Bay lighthouse.

Charlotte Pass is a cold spot.

NSW floral emblem: Waratah.

DID YOU KNOW?

City on a Harbour

FACTS

▶ Sydney has over 750 suburbs and is home to over 3 850 000 people (20% of Australia's population).

▶ Sydney is on a great sandstone shelf which was formed 180–225 million years ago.

▶ The Parramatta and Lane Cove Rivers carry little silt into Sydney Harbour, so its water is quite clear.

▶ Sydney is almost completely surrounded by national parks and bushland.

▶ Sydney's hottest recorded day was 45.3°C on 14.1.1931.

Rollerblader at Bondi beach.

An aerial view of Sydney Harbour with the cruise liner *Oriana* escorted by small craft.

Manly, one of Sydney's famous ocean beaches.

Sydney is Australia's largest and oldest city, founded in 1788 as a place of exile for British convicts. Those first people from Britain struggled to adapt to the land and climate. Today, Sydney is a world famous city standing on a magnificent harbour. It is Australia's oldest and largest city, home to people who come from countries all over the world, as well as many indigenous Australians.

1	Farm Cove	9	The Domain
2	Kirribilli	10	Circular Quay
3	Kings Cross	11	Hyde Park
4	Opera House	12	Sydney Harbour Bridge
5	Royal Botanic Gardens	13	Cahill Expressway
6	Government House	14	Sydney Tower
7	Woolloomooloo	15	The Rocks
8	Bradfield Highway	16	Dawes Point Park
		17	Botany Bay

◄ SYDNEY HARBOUR

Is an ancient river valley flooded when an ice age ended. Has over 300 km of shoreline. North and South Heads guard 1.5-km-wide entrance. Circular Quay is the terminus for Harbour ferries.

SYDNEY HARBOUR BRIDGE ▶

Took 8 years to build. Opened 1932. Traffic deck is 59 m above water. Arch spans 503 m, top is 134 m above water. Weighs 52 732 tonnes. More than 150 000 vehicles cross daily.

◄ SYDNEY OPERA HOUSE

Designed by Jørn Utzon. Begun 1959, opened 1973. Covers 1.8 ha of Bennelong Point. Highest point 67 m above Harbour. Concert hall seats 2690. Yearly attendances 1.5 million.

THE ROCKS ▶

Where the First Fleet settlers set up camp near the Tank Stream in 1788. During the 1800s became a sleazy dockside slum. Today has historic buildings, markets, galleries, museums and Observatory Hill.

SYDNEY ▶ TOWER

Opened 1981. Tallest building in the Southern Hemisphere. The top of its 30-m spire is 305 m above street level. The nine-level turret can hold 1000 people, has an observation level and cafes and restaurants.

▲ DARLING HARBOUR

Disused harbourside area redeveloped for Sydney's 1988 Bicentenary. Covers 54 ha. Site of Maritime, Powerhouse Museums, Harbourside Marketplace, Sydney Aquarium, Chinese Garden.

FACTS

▶ It took 1400 men to construct the Harbour Bridge. Sixteen of them died in accidents.

▶ Utzon modelled the framework of each of the 10 Opera House roofs on the way the fronds of a palm leaf fan from the main stem.

▶ Suez Canal in The Rocks was once called Sewer's Canal after its open drains.

▶ Each of Sydney Tower's 56 cables weighs 7 tonnes. The lifts in the tower take only 40 seconds to pass 76 floors to the Observation Level. There are 2 staircases, each with 1474 steps. Runners race up these each October.

Taronga Park is Sydney's world-famous Zoo.

Blue Mountains to Border Ranges

DID YOU KNOW?

FACTS

▶ The Zig-Zag Railway, up Mt Victoria in the Blue Mts, was constructed 1866–69. Replaced by a ten-tunnel line in 1910, it now carries tourists reliving the glorious days of steam trains.

▶ The Jenolan Caves became famous after a bushranger called James McKeown was captured hiding out there in 1838.

▶ In 1994 the discovery of a tree whose fossil record dates back 160 million years was announced. Just 39 specimens of the Wollemi Pine had been found in one valley in Wollemi NP. It is now being ᴳcloned at Sydney's Royal Botanic Gardens.

The Great Dividing Range sweeps from the Blue Mountains, west of Sydney, northwards to the Queensland border.

Swift rivers make their way to the sea on the east of the watershed, and other slower ones flow west to join the Murray–Darling river systems.

Up to 30 million years ago, there was great volcanic activity in this area. It left rich, weathered ᴳbasalt soil and high peaks whose tops were protected by basalt caps, such as Point Lookout (1564 m), Round Mountain (1586 m), Chandlers Peak (1473 m) and Mt Warning (1156 m).

THE MOUNTAINS ARE NOT AS BLUE AS THEY SEEM

The Three Sisters and a Katoomba Skyway cable car.

BLUE MOUNTAINS SITES & SIGHTS
- The Three Sisters
- The Jamison Valley
- Katoomba Skyway
- Leura Cascades
- Govetts Leap
- Zig Zag Railway
- Scenic Railway
- Mt Tomah Gardens
- Wentworth Falls
- Jenolan Caves
- Cathedral of Ferns

Rising 105 km west of Sydney, the Blue Mountains are full of sheer sandstone cliffs, rugged gorges and dense forests. The mountains appear blue because of the haze produced by light glancing off fine droplets of oil given off by the leaves of eucalypt trees.

Crystal Showers Falls, Dorrigo NP. *Inset:* Spotted-tailed Quoll.

Where wild rivers run

Dorrigo, Guy Fawkes River and Oxley Wild Rivers National Parks have some of Australia's most spectacular scenery.

For many years the rainforests of northern NSW were cleared for timber and farms. Clashes between loggers and ᴳconservationists led to eight remnant areas of warm temperate rainforest being listed as a World Heritage Area: the Central Eastern Rainforest Reserves.

"Country" country

The New England Tableland lies in the north-east of NSW to the west of the Great Divide. It is about 130 km wide and around 1000 m above sea level.

In the 1830s, the first sheep farmers named the area after their homeland. They planted northern hemisphere trees whose leaves colour in autumn. Today the tableland is noted for wool, fat lambs and beef. Armidale has a university and famous schools. Tamworth is the country music capital of Australia — a ten-day Country Festival has been held there each January since 1973. The Fossickers Way takes gemstone seekers from Tamworth to Inverell and Glen Innes.

Bald Rock is 1112 m high and 750 m long.

BORN FROM EARTH'S FIERY HEART

The Warrumbungle Mountains are popular with bushwalkers and climbers.

The Breadknife was once a blade of molten rock.

Mt Warning, core of an ancient volcano.

A line of volcanoes once stretched 800 km from Kingaroy, Qld, to Orange and Oberon, NSW. The Warrumbungle Mountains are the remains of a volcano some 50 km wide which was active between 17 and 13 million years ago. Much of the Tweed Volcano, in north-eastern NSW, has weathered away to leave the harder central plug of solidified ᴳlava known today as Mt Warning.

15

Central Coast to Northern Rivers

FACTS

- In 1824, Scots engineer John Busby arrived in NSW to construct Sydney's first water supply. His son James planted vines from France and Spain at John Busby's Kirkton property, sharing in the start of the wine industry in the Hunter Valley.

- In 1855, a Hunter Valley wine was presented to French Emperor Napoleon III. Paris Exhibition judges named it a fine wine.

- At Wingen, Burning Mountain, in the Upper Hunter Valley, smoke pours out of vents in the ground. It comes from underground seams of coal which have been burning for up to 6000 years.

The coastal area between Sydney and the Queensland border has reliable, abundant summer rainfall. Many rivers flow from the Great Dividing Range to the Pacific Ocean. Their flood plains are covered with rich soil and their estuaries make fine harbours and good places to catch fish.

The eastern slopes of the Great Dividing Range were once covered with rainforest. In northern NSW much has been cleared, but some areas are protected in national parks. Many people make a living here farming or fishing, in coal mining or industry, or in the hospitality industry looking after holiday-makers and tourists who flock to seaside resorts and mountain getaways.

The Platypus lives in coastal rivers.

The Entrance guards the opening to Tuggerah Lakes, three adjoining waterways.

Central Coast towns are great places to fish and enjoy water sports.

Riches of vine and mine

The valley of the Hunter River produces some of the world's best wines. More than 70 wineries welcome visitors to taste and buy. The Hunter Valley also produces high-grade coal and electricity, and is home to some famous thoroughbred horse studs. The port of Newcastle is Australia's sixth-largest city and a great industrial centre.

Pepper Tree Wines is one of the Hunter Valley's many wineries.

Queens Wharf, Newcastle, is a popular place to eat, walk and enjoy the sea.

Pelicans are common on the north coast of NSW.

GONE FISHIN'

The northern coast of NSW offers great fishing in rivers and estuaries, off beaches and rocks, and out to sea. Some fish live all their lives in one area, others migrate each year.

Coastline in Yuraygir National Park.

WILD GREEN PLACES

Coastal national parks include Booti Booti, Bongil Bongil, Yuraygir and Bundjalung. Inland, nature runs wild in national parks such as Oxley Wild Rivers, New England and Nightcap.

Tiger Snake venom is milked at Gosford Reptile Park.

THE HOLIDAY COAST

From Manly to Tweed Heads, the northern coast is packed full of great golden surf beaches, fish-filled estuaries, sea and shore birds, top seaside resorts and happy holiday-makers.

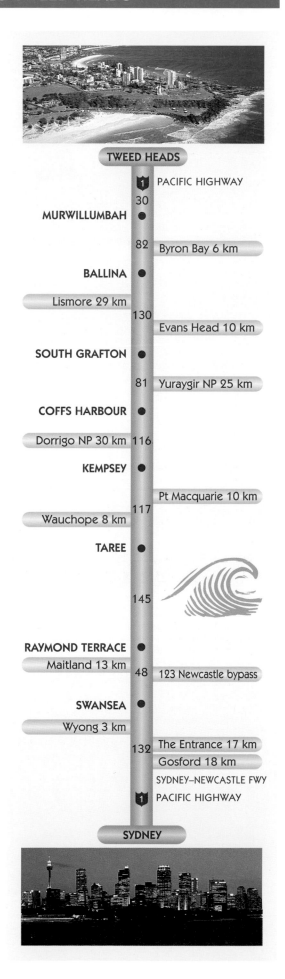

TWEED HEADS

1 PACIFIC HIGHWAY
30
MURWILLUMBAH
82 Byron Bay 6 km
BALLINA
Lismore 29 km
130 Evans Head 10 km
SOUTH GRAFTON
81 Yuraygir NP 25 km
COFFS HARBOUR
Dorrigo NP 30 km 116
KEMPSEY
Pt Macquarie 10 km
117
Wauchope 8 km
TAREE
145
RAYMOND TERRACE
Maitland 13 km
48 123 Newcastle bypass
SWANSEA
Wyong 3 km
132 The Entrance 17 km
Gosford 18 km
SYDNEY–NEWCASTLE FWY
1 PACIFIC HIGHWAY

SYDNEY

FACTS

▶ Each summer, NSW advances all clocks one hour to Summer Time. Qld does not. This means Tweed Heads (NSW) is one hour ahead of next-door Coolangatta (Qld).

▶ At Coffs Harbour, a breakwater links the mainland to Muttonbird Island, where up to 30 000 shearwaters nest in burrows each year. They visit their chicks only at night.

▶ At Newcastle Beach is the Bogey Hole, a swimming pool carved from rock by convicts for their supervisor, Major James Morisset.

▶ Old Sydney Town at Gosford recreates Sydney 1788–1806. Actors portray everyday life of the era, including floggings.

▶ The Australian Reptile Park in North Gosford was established by Eric Worrell. Its displays include crocodiles, snakes, lizards and platypuses. Venomous snakes are milked each mid-afternoon. The venom is used to make antivenene, a substance to counteract the effects of snakebite.

Sydney to the Alps

FACTS

▶ Wollongong is the third largest city in NSW. Its name means "sound of the sea".

▶ At Blowhole Point, near Kiama, wave action forces seawater up to 60 m into the air.

▶ On Stanwell Park beach, north of Wollongong, Lawrence Hargraves was the first Australian to rise off the ground (nearly 5 m) using heavier than air equipment (4 box kites tethered on top of each other) in 1894.

▶ Cricketer Don Bradman was raised in Bowral and at age 12 scored his first century for Bowral High School. He went on to make a 99.94-run Test average.

▶ Each night at Glow Worm Glen, near Bundanoon, tiny gnat ᴳlarvae glow to lure insect prey into their webs. The hungrier a "glow worm", the brighter it shines.

▶ Kangaroo Valley's Hampden Bridge replaced a convict-built wooden bridge in 1898. Five days after it was opened, the old bridge was washed away by floods.

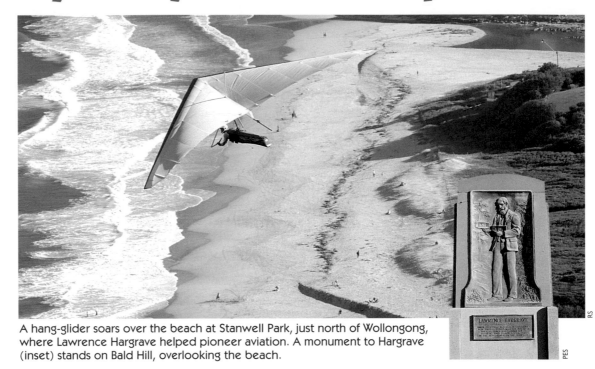

A hang-glider soars over the beach at Stanwell Park, just north of Wollongong, where Lawrence Hargrave helped pioneer aviation. A monument to Hargrave (inset) stands on Bald Hill, overlooking the beach.

The route from Sydney to Canberra passes through the very "English" Southern Highlands.

Goulburn, at the southern end of the Highlands, was once a base for bushranger-hunting police troopers. Today it boasts the Big Merino, a hollow statue of a sheep, 15 m high.

Wollongong is an hour's drive south of Sydney. The area produces high-grade coal, and Port Kembla, just to the south, has Australia's largest steelworks and one of the world's largest ᴳblast furnaces.

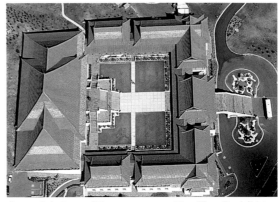

An aerial view of the enormous Nan Tien Buddhist temple, near Wollongong.

The Southern Highlands

This area is 650–860 m above sea level and is around 110 km south-west of Sydney, on the tableland to the east of Wollongong.

The cool winter climate of the Highlands means European plants flourish and the town of Bowral holds a colourful Tulip Time festival in September. The region holds a cold-weather "Christmas" festival each June–July. Kangaroo Valley is a fertile rural area which is so full of history that the whole valley is classified by the National Trust.

Hampden Bridge, Kangaroo Valley.

Meeting Eastern Grey Kangaroos at Murramarang NP.

Eden killers, Bega cheeses

Beaches, great surf, water sports and fishing fleets combine to make the South Coast of NSW a great place to spend seaside holidays.

It is also a fine place to bushwalk in wild places, see wildlife (kangaroos roam the beach in Murramarang NP), to visit Central Tilba historic village, eat up at Bega Cheese Factory and visit the Eden Killer Whale Museum.

High, white and handsome

The Snowy Mountains are a playground for winter snow-sporters and summer holiday-makers.

Kosciuszko National Park, the largest national park in NSW, surrounds ski resorts such as Thredbo Village, Perisher and Smiggin Holes. The Skitube mostly underground railway travels from Bullocks Flat, near Jindabyne, to Charlotte Pass (8 km from the summit of Mt Kosciuszko) and Blue Cow Mountain.

Common Wombat

Winter landscape in Kosciuszko NP.

OTHER STATES' HIGHEST
TAS: Mt Ossa 1617 m
QLD: Mt Bartle Frere 1622 m
NT: Mt Zeil 1531 m
SA: Mt Woodroffe 1435 m
WA: Mt Meharry 1249 m

AUSTRALIA'S HIGHEST PEAKS

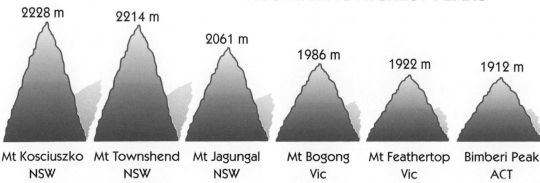

2228 m	2214 m	2061 m	1986 m	1922 m	1912 m
Mt Kosciuszko NSW	Mt Townshend NSW	Mt Jagungal NSW	Mt Bogong Vic	Mt Feathertop Vic	Bimberi Peak ACT

West of the Divide

FACTS

▶ Two-thirds of Australia's irrigated land is along the Murray and its tributaries. Irrigating crops uses 75% of NSW's total water resources.

▶ Salt and blue-green algae are threats to water-use from the Murray–Darling system. Introduced fish threaten native fish.

▶ Wagga Wagga on the Murrumbidgee River, is NSW's largest inland city.

▶ Gumly Gumly, near Wagga Wagga, boasts a Murray Cod hatchery whose star, magnificent Big Murray, is more than 100 years old and weighs over 50 kg.

▶ Before Europeans arrived, the area around Deniliquin was rich in bush tucker and was probably the most densely populated place in Australia.

Good eating – Murray crays.

Cattle being moved along a road near Gunnedah, on the plains west of the Great Dividing Range.

In New South Wales, the Great Dividing Range varies from 50–160 km in width. On its western side, it slopes gradually to vast plains which cover almost two-thirds of the State.

These plains are drained by the Murray–Darling river complex, Australia's longest river system and the only inland waterway to flow all year round (more on the Murray on p. 35). Much of the far west is arid, where small towns service cattle and sheep properties, and large towns exist because of mining.

Irrigated croplands and sandhills show two faces of the land bordering the Murray River.

Dunes and clues

Mungo National Park is in the dry country north-east of Mildura.

Over 40 000 years ago this was a lake bordered by a long sand dune. On the lake's shores lived many Aborigines. The climate changed, the lake dried up and today only bones of humans and animals, stone tools and sand-buried camps give clues to a vanished way of life. The remains of the dune, now a half-moon of wind-carved sand, is called The Walls of China.

Sand formations in Mungo NP.

Wild on the plains

The Western Plains Zoo, a sister-zoo to Taronga Park, is near Dubbo, 482 km west of Sydney.

Here animals from many countries, including Australia, roam in large areas and can be admired across waterways and from a network of roads.

Rhinoceros and zebra at Western Plains Zoo.

The back of beyond

Graziers in western NSW have to be careful not to overstock their runs following good rains, because drought will surely come again.

Sheep and cattle can be raised in ᴳarid country using water from the Great Artesian Basin, a natural underground reservoir.

The game's the same, in Sydney or the bush.

Stockhorse race at an Outback race meeting.

MINING AND MIMING

Today the biggest mining centres in western NSW are Cobar (copper-lead-zinc-silver) and Broken Hill (silver-lead-zinc). Cobar survives on water piped 110 km from the Bogan River. Broken Hill's streets are named after minerals and it is a home for many artists. Nearby Silverton is a ghost town which is famous as a film, TV commercials and TV series location.

The Silverton Hotel, where mining history meets showbiz.

Black opal from Lightning Ridge.

Lightning Ridge, in north-western NSW, is the world's largest source of fine black opals. The town has an underground showroom and cinema. At White Cliffs, an opal town near Broken Hill, miners live underground.

21

FACTS

- Canberra is 577 m above sea level.

- Canberra is on the limestone plains of the Molonglo River, which is a ᵉtributary of the Murrumbidgee River.

- Canberra is Australia's foggiest capital city.

- Namadgi NP covers about 40% of the ACT. It links up with Kosciuszko NP, NSW, which adjoins Alpine NP in Victoria.

- Federal Parliament meets in Canberra. It is made up of 76 Senators and 148 members of the House of Representatives .

- The ACT has governed itself only since 1989. It has a single Lower House made up of 17 elected members.

- Walter Burley Griffin's design for Canberra won a $3500 prize in 1912. Rejected by a government board which wanted its own plan used, it was reinstated after 800 architects and engineers petitioned the government.

- Australia's External Territories include the Australian Antarctic Territory, Norfolk Is, Heard Is, Macquarie Is, and Christmas Is.

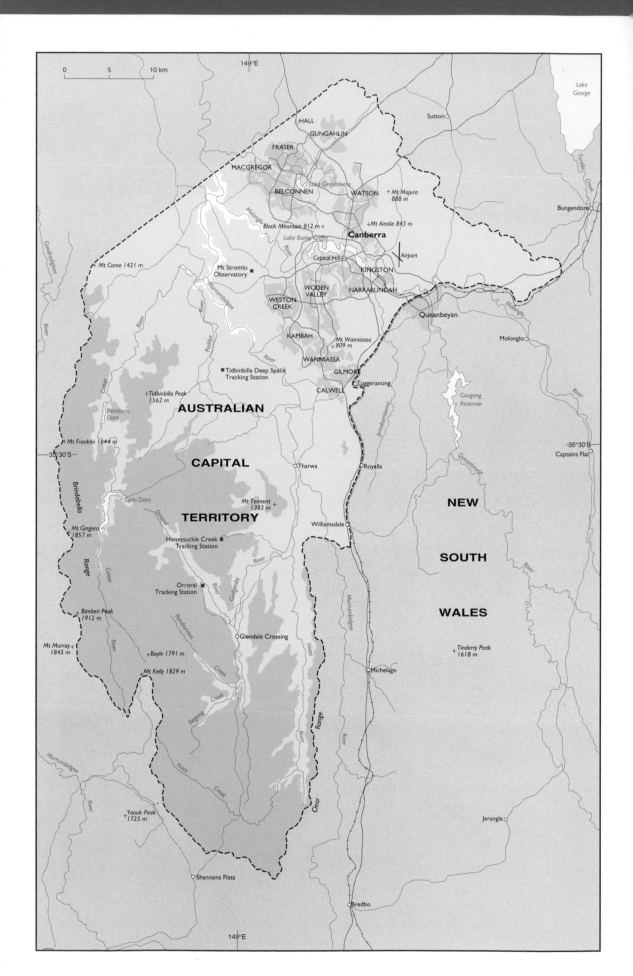

For the Queen, the Law, and the People.

	Jan	Apr	Jul	Oct
max °C	28	20	11	19
min °C	13	7	0	6
rainfall mm	58	49	40	68
rainy days	8	8	10	11

Eastern Grey Kangaroos at Tidbinbilla Nature Reserve, ACT.

The flag of the Australian Capital Territory.

THE NATIONAL CAPITAL

In 1911, an area on the plains of the Molonglo River halfway between Sydney and Melbourne was acquired by the ten-year-old Commonwealth Government as a site for the Australian Capital Territory. The city of Canberra was planned by Walter Burley Griffin and construction began in 1913. Fifty years later, a dam across the Molonglo created Lake Burley Griffin and completed Burley Griffin's vision for the city. Jervis Bay, 150 km to the east, gives the ACT a sea port.

The Canberra Coat of Arms features a black and a white swan supporting a shield on which are a castle, the Sword of Justice and a ᴳmace. Above the shield are a gate, a crown and a gum tree. The motto beneath the shield is "For the Queen, the Law and the People".

KNOW MORE ABOUT THE AUSTRALIAN CAPITAL TERRITORY

Total area: 2 400 km²
% of area of Aust: 0.03
Coastline length: 35 km
Population: 331 800

Highest point: Bimberi Peak (1912 m)
Highest rainfall in one day: 105 mm on 21.10.1959

Coldest: -15.1°C (ground temperature) on 11.7.1971
Hottest: 42.8°C on 11.1.1939
Longest river: Murrumbidgee

ᴳ**Floral emblem:** Royal Bluebell
ᴳ**Faunal emblem:** Gang-Gang Cockatoo

Jervis Bay is part of the ACT.

Springtime in Canberra.

Canberra winters are very cold.

Male Gang-Gang Cockatoo.

A meeting place

Walter Burley Griffin's plan placed many of Canberra's most important buildings within a "parliamentary triangle" formed by Kings Avenue, Commonwealth Avenue and Lake Burley Griffin. Parliament House, Old Parliament House, the National Library, the High Court, Questacon and the Australian National Gallery are in this triangle. On the northern side of the lake are Canberra city, Commonwealth Park, and Anzac Parade which leads to the Australian War Memorial at the foot of 842-m Mt Ainslie.

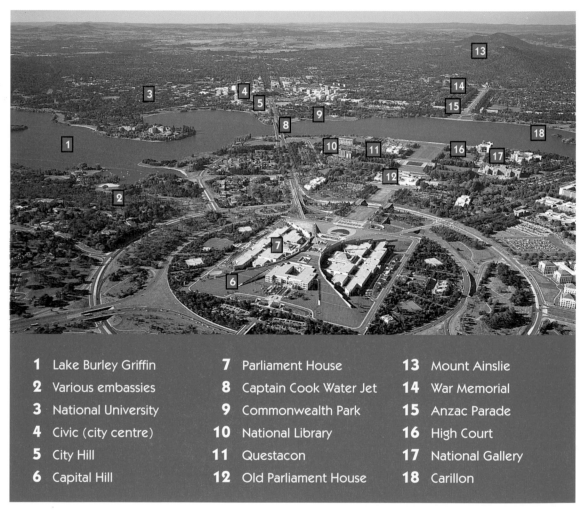

1	Lake Burley Griffin	7	Parliament House	13	Mount Ainslie
2	Various embassies	8	Captain Cook Water Jet	14	War Memorial
3	National University	9	Commonwealth Park	15	Anzac Parade
4	Civic (city centre)	10	National Library	16	High Court
5	City Hill	11	Questacon	17	National Gallery
6	Capital Hill	12	Old Parliament House	18	Carillon

DID YOU KNOW?

FACTS

▶ From 1913–28 Canberra was "dry". People who wanted to drink alcohol had to travel 11 km to Queanbeyan, across the NSW border.

▶ Hot air balloons are a feature of the autumn Canberra Festival. Half a million visitors enjoy the Floriade flower festival each springtime.

Canberra's oldest building, Blundell's Farmhouse (1860).

"Stonehenge" in the miniature English village at Cockington Green, ACT.

Our House

Parliament House stands on Capital Hill. This building belongs to the people of Australia, and it is open to the public 364 days every year. It cost $1.1 billion, took 8 years to build, and was opened in 1988.

Many of its 4500 rooms are underground and the public can walk across its grassed-over roof. The open space in front of the building has a mosaic based on Aboriginal themes.

In front of Parliament House is the Great Verandah. The mosaic has over 100 000 pieces of granite.

SOME CANBERRA LANDMARKS

◄ LAKE BURLEY GRIFFIN

Area 7 km². Average depth 4.5 m, shoreline 36 km. Captain Cook Water Jet is 137 m high and jet weighs 6 tonnes. Carillon's 53 bells weigh from 7 kg to 6 tonnes. Acton is base for boat and cycle hire.

THE TELSTRA TOWER ►

Stands on Black Mountain, which is 812 m high. Tower is 195.2 m high. Viewing galleries are at 66.1 m level. Revolving restaurant is at 54.0 m level. Transmits TVs/radios/mobile phones. Public can enter tower from 9 a.m. to 10 p.m. every day.

◄ INSTITUTE OF SPORT

Near Black Mountain Reserve. Founded 1981. Athletes lead daily public tours. Courts and pools used by public. Sportex is hands-on sports display.

QUESTACON ►

National Science and Technology Centre. Hands-on interactive displays about science in everyday life. Built 1988 as joint project with Japan. Drum tower is 27 m high.

AUSTRALIAN ► WAR MEMORIAL

Designed 1925, opened 1941. Contains 1 million photos, 40 000 relics, 20 000 maps, etc. Unknown Soldier lies in Hall of Memory. Most visited Canberra building.

FACTS

▶ Amongst names suggested for Australia's capital were Meladneyperbane, Cooeeton and Kangermu.

▶ "Canberry" is an Aboriginal word meaning either "meeting place" or "breasts" (referring to the area's hills).

▶ Canberra has an area of 805 km². Around 30% of its residents work for the government.

▶ Tidbinbilla Deep Space Communications Complex is 40 km from Canberra.

Exhibit at the National Dinosaur Museum.

A figure from the Navy Memorial in Anzac Parade.

VICTORIA

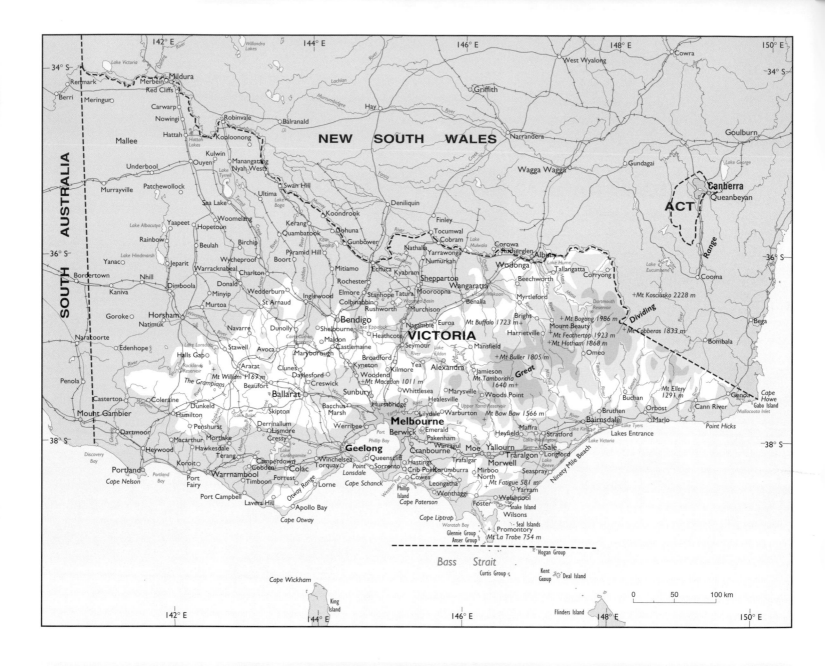

FACTS FACTS FACTS FACTS FACTS FACTS FACTS FACTS FACTS FACTS FACTS FACTS FACTS

▸ The first European to see the Victorian coast was Lieut. Zachary Hicks, of Captain Cook's *Endeavour*. On 20 April 1770 he spotted a cape which Captain Cook named Point Hicks in his honour.

▸ Rich gold strikes at Ballarat and Bendigo in 1851 made Victoria prosperous.

▸ Australia's only armed rebellion took place on the Ballarat goldfields, at the Eureka Stockade in 1854.

▸ Australian Rules Football originated in Victoria. Played by 2 teams of 18, a game lasts for 100 minutes.

▸ At the 1956 Melbourne Olympics, Australians won 35 medals.

▸ Around 23% of Australia's farm products, including beef, wool, wheat oats and barley, come from Victoria.

▸ The largest Victorian country towns are Geelong, Ballarat and Bendigo.

▸ Victorian tourist attractions include Phillip Island, the Dandenongs, the Gippsland Lakes, Alpine NP, the Victorian goldfields, the Great Ocean Road, the Grampians and the Murray River.

BENDIGO'S CLIMATE				
	Jan	Apr	Jul	Oct
max °C	29	21	12	20
min °C	14	9	3	8
rainfall mm	34	41	56	53
rainy days	5	7	13	10

MELBOURNE'S CLIMATE				
	Jan	Apr	Jul	Oct
max °C	26	20	13	20
min °C	14	11	6	9
rainfall mm	48	57	49	67
rainy days	8	12	15	14

PEACEFUL AND PROSPEROUS

White settlers arrived in Victoria in 1834. The colony separated from NSW in 1851, at the time gold was discovered near Ballarat and Bendigo. Today Victoria is Australia's smallest mainland State, but encompasses a wide range of landscapes and offers many opportunities for adventure. The list of places to see and to explore includes the historic Goldfields towns, wild Wilsons Promontory, beautiful Gippsland, the alpine High Country, the south-western coastline, the Grampians and the Murray River.

Victoria's Coat of Arms has a blue shield, which carries the five stars of the Southern Cross, supported by two female figures. One, representing Peace, holds an olive branch, the other, representing Prosperity, supports a cornucopia (horn of plenty).

The flag of Victoria.

On the crest above the shield, on a wreath of silver and blue, a kangaroo holds an Imperial Crown between its paws. The State motto is "Peace and Prosperity".

KNOW MORE ABOUT VICTORIA

Area: 227 600 km²
Length of seacoast: 1800 km
Population: 4 503 400
Most southerly point of mainland: South East Point

Highest point: Mt Bogong (1986 m)
Highest annual rainfall: 3738 mm at Falls Creek, Victorian Alps, in 1956

Coldest recorded: -12.8° at Mt Hotham on 30.7.1931
Hottest recorded: 50.8° at Mildura, on the Murray River, on 6.1.1906

Floral emblem: Common Heath
Faunal emblem: Leadbeater's Possum, Helmeted Honeyeater

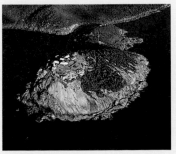

South East Point.

Mt Bogong.

Murray River bridge, Mildura.

Leadbeater's Possum.

FACTS

- ▶ Melbourne's hottest day on record was 13.1.1939, when it reached 45.6°C.

- ▶ Melbourne Central has a 20-storey glass cone protecting an old shot tower. Lumps of molten lead were dropped from the tower. The fall shaped them into rounds to be fired from muzzle-loading guns.

- ▶ The cottage in which Captain Cook's parents lived in the 1750s was brought from Yorkshire, UK, to Fitzroy Gardens.

- ▶ Melbourne has Australia's only tram network. Early trams were called "the green thunderers". Modern ones are much quieter.

MELBOURNE, CAPITAL OF VICTORIA

City on the Yarra

Tram and Melbourne Central.

The old Shot Tower.

Melbourne was founded in the 1830s on land acquired from the Aboriginal people by John Batman and John Fawkner.

Today, Melbourne is Australia's second-largest city. Standing on the northern shores of Port Phillip Bay, it is famous for its gardens and as a business centre. Melburnians enjoy art, other culture and sport. There are four things which symbolise Melbourne — the Yarra River, the city's electric trams, Australian Rules football and Australia's richest horse race, the annual Melbourne Cup.

The Yarra River winds through Melbourne. Government House stands in the Royal Botanic Gardens.

1	St Kilda Pier	10	Lygon & Victoria Sts
2	Albert Park Lake	11	Exhibition Centre
3	Vic Arts Centre	12	Melbourne Central
4	Southgate Complex	13	City Baths
5	St Pauls Cathedral	14	Carlton
6	Carlton Gardens	15	Williamstown
7	Port Phillip Bay	16	Port Melbourne
8	Crown Casino	17	Yarra River
9	State Library	18	Flagstaff Gardens

SOME MELBOURNE LANDMARKS

◄ SOUTHGATE

On Yarra River's bank over Princes Bridge from Flinders Street Station. Popular place to shop, eat out. Near Crown Casino. Victorian Arts Centre is on St Kilda Road just past Southgate. Across St Kilda Rd are Queen Victoria Gardens and Kings Domain. Yarra cruises leave nearby.

MELBOURNE ZOO ►

Opened 1862. Home to more than 350 different sorts of animals. Most popular animals include Lowland Gorillas (*right*), Lesser Pandas (*far right*), tigers, otters and koalas. Partner zoo at Werribee is free-range.

◄ SCIENCEWORKS

Located in Spotswood at mouth of Yarra River. Is a high-tech branch of the Museum of Victoria. Contains many hands-on exhibits with scientific themes. Includes Sportsworks section.

▼ VICTORIAN ARTS CENTRE

In St Kilda Rd. Includes National Gallery of Victoria, theatres, concert hall. Angel (*below*) by Deborah Halpern stands in front of the Gallery.

▲ FLINDERS STREET STATION

Built 1899–1910. Popular meeting place. Hub of suburban rail lines. Clocks above entrance show train departure times.

FACTS

▶ Melbourne's Old Gaol was the scene of Ned Kelly's hanging in 1880. Pentridge Gaol saw Australia's last execution, that of Ronald Ryan, in 1967.

▶ The Melbourne Cup is run at Flemington on the first Tuesday of November each year.

▶ The most popular exhibit in the Museum of Victoria is the stuffed body of legendary racehorse Phar Lap.

▶ The Melbourne Cricket Ground (MCG) holds more than 90 000 spectators. It is used for cricket, football and concerts.

▶ The first England-Australia Cricket Test took place at the MCG in 1877. Australia won.

▶ The World Health Organisation rates Melbourne as one of the world's least polluted cities.

▶ Because it is home to many people of Greek background, Melbourne has been called "the world's third-largest Greek city".

East of Melbourne

Australian Fur-seal.

Koala at Healesville Sanctuary, 65 km from Melbourne.

The Mornington Peninsula is the eastern arm of Port Phillip Bay. Its outer shores border Western Port and Bass Strait.

From St Kilda and Brighton to Portsea, the bay has plenty of beaches, holiday resorts, good swimming, fishing and sailing. The wilder eastern ocean side is enjoyed by surfers, divers and people who like fishing spiced with adventure.

The Bay, the Peninsula and Bass Strait.

Penguins on parade

It is a 120-km drive from Melbourne down the Bass Highway to Phillip Island.

Many people go to see the evening "parade" of Little Penguins returning to their nests at Summerland Beach. Others enjoy seal-watching from boats, or through telescopes set up on the Nobbies. Visitors to Phillip Island can also meet Koalas at the Koala Conservation Centre.

Little Penguins.

A GREEN PLACE NEAR THE CITY

Puffing Billy carries sightseers through the ranges.

Fifty kilometres west of Melbourne, the Dandenong Ranges have been a green refuge from the city for over 100 years. The ranges are famous for colourful cool-climate gardens and a national park which protects magnificent forests and wildlife. The steam train Puffing Billy chugs and toots between Belgrave and the Emerald Lakeside Park.

Down on the Prom

Wilsons Promontory, which is about 170 km south-east of Melbourne, has been a national park since 1905. For bushwalkers, nature lovers and people who enjoy the sea, "The Prom" is a wonderful place to be.

The sand at Squeaky Bay on Wilsons Promontory is so fine that it "sings" as someone walks across it.

THE VICTORIAN HIGH COUNTRY

Taking the easy way up a mountain.

Mt Buffalo stands in its own national park.

Victoria's High Country is the southern end of the mainland's Great Dividing Range. In winter, ski resorts attract big crowds, while summer belongs to walkers, anglers, climbers and campers.

Lakes Entrance, the opening in Ninety Mile Beach which connects the Gippsland Lakes and Bass Strait.

Glorious Gippsland

Gippsland is the area between the Great Dividing Range, Westernport Bay and the Lakes District.

There is coal in the Latrobe Valley, rainforest in the ranges, dairy and other farms and marvellous beaches for all to enjoy around the Lakes District. Tarra-Bulga National Park is the place to see tall trees and Superb Lyrebirds.

Lifesavers on Ninety Mile Beach.

High and mighty

The ranges of south-eastern Victoria are home to the world's tallest flowering tree, the Mountain Ash.

The tallest Mountain Ash reliably recorded was felled at Watts River in 1872. Its trunk was 132.6 m high and its topmost leaves probably reached 150 m above the ground.

A stand of Mountain Ash in Gippsland.

Gold, surf and shipwreck

Gold was discovered at Ballarat and Bendigo in 1851. During the 1850s, around 90% of Australia's total production of gold came from Victoria.

Money and migrants poured into the colony. Goldrush towns such as Ballarat, Bendigo, Ararat, Castlemaine and Stawell became prosperous and

Replica of the Eureka Stockade.

their residents built impressive stone buildings, monuments and parks. In 1854, Ballarat was the scene of the Eureka Stockade, where miners protesting against licence fees came into armed conflict with government troops.

Today, the goldfields towns preserve many reminders of the roaring days: Sovereign Hill at Ballarat recreates a town of the time; Stawell has a working open-cut mine; Bendigo's Central Deborah Mine has been restored and can be explored.

Sovereign Hill re-creates a goldrush town.

Ned Kelly was executed at Old Melbourne Gaol in November, 1880.

LEGEND IN ARMOUR

Ned Kelly, the son of an ex-convict, was born in 1855 at Beveridge, Victoria. His criminal career included horse and cattle theft, killing three policemen and holding up banks at Euroa and Jerilderie (NSW). Captured at Glenrowan in June 1880 after other gang members were killed, he was hanged in Melbourne Gaol on 11 November. He was 25.

City of Cats and wool

Geelong, Victoria's second-largest city, got its start during gold rush days and today is a major port and industrial centre.

It is also the home of a great Australian Rules Football team (the "Cats"), the National Wool Museum and over 100 historic buildings classified by the National Trust.

The National Wool Museum at Geelong.

Surfers and shipwrecks

The Great Ocean Road is said to be the finest scenic drive in the world.

It was hacked from the limestone cliffs by returned soldiers from 1919 to 1932 and completed with a section across Cape Otway in the 1980s. It gives access to magnificent surf beaches and overlooks the sites of many tragic shipwrecks.

The Great Ocean Road.

FACTS

▶ Victoria's oldest building, a small wooden customs house, was built in Sydney and erected in Geelong in 1838.

▶ The wreck of the *Cataraqui* on the Port Campbell coast in 1845 claimed 406 lives. In 1859, 94 died when the *Admella* sank. The 1878 *Loch Ard* disaster drowned 52.

THE GREAT OCEAN ROAD – GEELONG TO PORTLAND

In the Otway Ranges. *Inset:* Eastern Yellow Robin.

A top pro surfing event is held at Bells Beach.

GEELONG

100 SURFCOAST HIGHWAY

21

TORQUAY ●

16

ANGLESEA ● To Bells Beach

11

AIREYS INLET ●

To Angahook-Lorne SP 18

LORNE ●

45

APOLLO BAY ●

Otway NP — Otway NP

To Cape Otway

100 To Melba Gully SP

Otway NP — Port Campbell NP

PORT CAMPBELL ●

100 GREAT OCEAN RD

66

1 PRINCES HIGHWAY

WARRNAMBOOL ●

99

PORTLAND

This was known as the Shipwreck Coast.

Viewing the Twelve Apostles.

33

Mallee and Murray

FACTS

▶ Nhill, on the Western Hwy halfway between Melbourne and Adelaide, has the biggest grain silo in the Southern Hemisphere.

▶ Mt Arapiles (369 m) attracts rock-climbers from all over the world. Some of the routes up its sides are called "Delirium Tremens", "Anxiety Neurosis" and "Wall of Horrors".

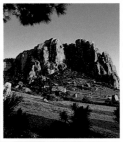

Mt Arapiles.

▶ Malleefowl heap sand and vegetation into a nest about 1.5 m high and 5 m across. The female lays eggs at intervals into the top of the mound, then the male piles sand over them. He tests the temperature with his beak daily and adds or removes sand to keep the egg chamber at 33°C.

▶ A Malleefowl chick digs its way up to the surface, then runs away from the nest. It looks after itself and has nothing to do with its parents.

The Grampians are the western end of the Great Dividing Range. Many Aborigines lived here when Major Thomas Mitchell arrived in the area in 1836. Today these sandstone ranges are favourites with wildlife-watchers, bushwalkers and rock-climbers.

This Grampians formation is called The Balconies, or The Jaws of Death.

Wimmera and Mallee

Central western Victoria is known as the Wimmera. Here huge wheat and sheep farms are interrupted by the Grampians and Mt Arapiles.

The north-western corner of Victoria is called the Mallee, after the many-trunked eucalypts which once covered the area. Much has been cleared to grow wheat and wool.

There are more than 2000 routes up Mt Arapiles.

WILDLIFE OF THE WIMMERA AND MALLEE

Mallee Fowl.

Red Kangaroos.

Emu.

THE MURRAY FROM SOURCE TO MOUTH

Above: A River Red Gum on a Murray backwater.
Below: Rafting on the Murray River.

The Murray River rises in the Snowy Mountains, NSW, and flows more than 2500 km to enter the sea at Lake Alexandrina, SA. With its tributary the Darling, it drains an area of more than 1 million km² (about one-seventh of Australia's total area). The Murray's catchment area has been largely stripped of trees, and dams and locks control its normal flow. Salt levels are rising, and this is a worry since it supplies water for drinking and household use and is used extensively for irrigation.

The Murray rises in the Snowy Mountains of NSW.

The Murray not far from its source.

Lake Hume, near Albury, has a 400-km shoreline.

A paddlewheeler on the Murray near Echuca.

Gliding over an irrigation area at Waikerie, SA.

Cattle graze on Lake Alexandrina's islands.

FACTS

▶ Most of the Murray River is in NSW, for the border lies along the southern bank.

▶ It may take 3 months for water to flow 2530 km from the Murray's source to its mouth. Four dams, including Hume Weir, hold back its progress.

▶ The Murray Cod may grow to almost 2 m and 100 kg. Over-fishing and competition from introduced European Carp have made it rare.

▶ An Aboriginal legend says the Murray was sung into existence by a man chasing a giant cod. The final struggle formed the Coorong and Lake Alexandrina.

▶ Until railways took over the transport of goods, paddlesteamers carried wool, timber and grain. Now they carry holiday-makers.

Paddlesteamer and Red Gum wharf at Echuca.

35

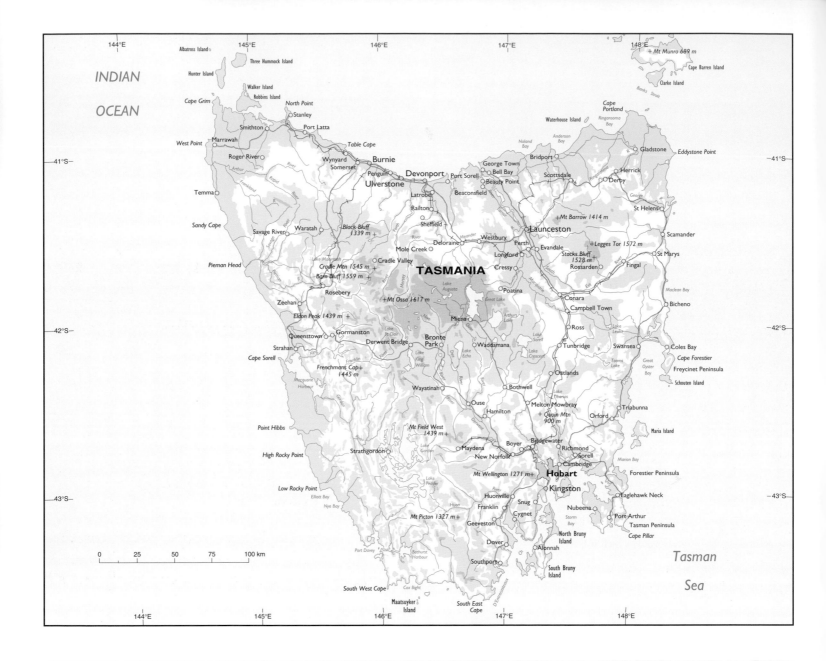

FACTS FACTS FACTS FACTS FACTS FACTS FACTS FACTS FACTS FACTS FACTS FACTS FACTS

▶ In 1642 Abel Tasman called this island Van Diemen's Land. In 1856, it was renamed Tasmania.

▶ During the first 35 years of European settlement, 183 Europeans and nearly 4000 Aborigines died.

▶ Today, more than 6500 descendants of the Tasmanian Aborigines still live in Tasmania.

▶ The Tasmanian Blue Gum was the first eucalypt described by a European, in 1642. It now grows worldwide.

▶ Tasmania's most popular tourist destinations include Hobart, Launceston, Port Arthur, Bicheno and Richmond. The many wilderness areas include Cradle Mtn-Lake St Clair, Franklin-Gordon Wild Rivers and Southwest NPs.

▶ 20% of Tasmania is World Heritage-listed, but its timber and water resources are very attractive to developers.

▶ Places on the west coast of Tasmania may receive more than 3 m of rain in a year.

▶ Tasmania is famous for wonderful food products, including seafood. The State is a world leader in farming fish such as Atlantic Salmon. Many rivers and lakes have been stocked with Rainbow and Brown Trout.

HOBART (south-east coast)				
	Jan	Apr	Jul	Oct
max °C	22	18	12	17
min °C	12	9	4	7
rainfall mm	37	49	49	48
rainy days	9	11	13	13

CRADLE MOUNTAIN (NW highlands)				
	Jan	Apr	Jul	Oct
max °C	17	11	5	10
min °C	6	4	0	2
rainfall mm	147	228	329	249
rainy days	16	20	24	21

THE ISLAND STATE

Tasmania was cut off from the Australian mainland by rising sea levels around 12 000 years ago. Its Aboriginal history goes back tens of thousands of years. Its much shorter European history includes a period in the early 1800s when it was a dreaded penal colony, Van Diemen's Land. Today Tasmania's rugged west and south-west, spectacular central plateau, fertile eastern farmland and splendid seacoast have earned the name "treasure island".

Tasmania's Coat of Arms reflects the State's British heritage and its industries. It shows two Thylacines (Tasmanian tigers) supporting a shield bearing a ram, a sheaf of wheat, apples, a branch of hops and a thunderbolt signifying ᴳhydro-electricity. Above the shield is a red lion, which has its origins in British ᴳheraldry, with a fore paw resting upon a

The flag of Tasmania.

pick and shovel, representing the Tasmanian mining industry. The motto, "Ubertas et Fidelitas", means "Fertility and Faithfulness".

KNOW MORE ABOUT TASMANIA

Total area: 67 800 km²
Coastline length: 3200 km
Population: 473 200
Highest point: Mt Ossa (1617 m)

Furthest point south: South Cape, lat. 43°39'S
Australia's record caves: 20 deepest and 5 longest caves are all in Tasmania

Coldest place: -13.0°C at Shannon on 30.6.1981
Australian record for least sunshine in one year: Tasmania's west coast

Floral emblem: Tasmanian Blue Gum
Unofficial faunal emblems: Tasmanian Devil and Yellow Wattlebird

Tasmania's southern coastline.

South Cape, Southwest NP.

Rainforest, western Tasmania.

Tasmanian Devil.

Hobart and the south

Hobart was settled in 1803, when the government in Sydney sent soldier and convicts there to protect British sealing and whaling interests.

Today Hobart stands on the estuary of the Derwent River, at the foot of Mt Wellington (1270 m). It has many reminders of the convict days, and of the early sailors, sealers and whalers who spent land-leave at places such as Battery Point. The warehouses of nearby Salamanca Place now are artists' studios, which form a background to weekend markets.

Hobart's waterfront is close to the city centre.

HOBART LANDMARKS

- Derwent River
- Mt Wellington
- The Wharf area
- Sullivans Cove
- Cadbury Chocolate Factory
- Old Penitentiary and Courts
- Cat and Fiddle Arcade
- Botanical Gardens
- Wrest Point Hotel-Casino
- Shot Tower, Taroona (1870)
- Battery Point
- Salamanca Place
- Anglesea Barracks (1811+)
- Kangaroo Bluff Forts (1880)

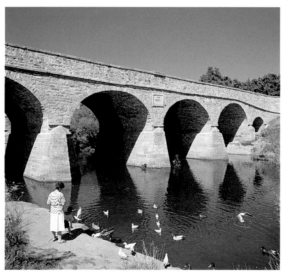

Richmond Bridge (1823) is said to be haunted by the ghost of a cruel overseer murdered by convicts.

FACTS

▸ Yachts leave Sydney each Boxing Day and race to Hobart. Their crews are honoured at a New Year's Eve party on Constitution Dock.

The Tasman Bridge.

▸ Hobart's Tasman Bridge was rammed by a cargo vessel in 1975. Repairs took 2 years.

▸ The deepest cave in Australia is Anne-A-Kananda (373 m), near Mt Anne west of Hobart. Exit Cave at Ida Bay, south of Hobart, is 17 km in length and is Australia's longest cave.

▸ The historic town of Richmond's stone bridge is the oldest in Australia.

▸ The convict Daniel Herbert earned a pardon by carving 186 designs in the Ross Bridge in 1836.

Carvings on the Ross Bridge include Celtic designs and portraits.

1	Princes Park
2	Battery Point
3	Salamanca Place
4	Princes Wharf
5	St Davids Park
6	Parliament Square
7	Murray St Pier
8	Brooke St Pier
9	Sullivans Cove
10	Franklin Square
11	Elizabeth St Pier
12	Tasmanian Museum
13	Constitution Dock
14	Franklin Wharf
15	Victoria Dock

World Heritage Tasmania

Western and central Tasmanian wilderness is known the world over.

Since 1982, six areas have been World Heritage listed: they are Southwest, Franklin-Gordon Wild Rivers, Cradle Mountain-Lake St Clair, Hartz Mts and the Walls of Jerusalem NPs, and the Central Plateau Protected Area.

Rugged scenery in Southwest NP.

A never-ending battle

Tasmania has been the scene for some fierce conservation battles.

In 1972 Lake Pedder was flooded to make hydro-electricity. The Tasmanian Government then tried to dam the lower Gordon and Franklin rivers. "Greenies" ᴳblockaded the construction and the police arrested 1400. In 1983, a new Federal Labor Government stopped the dam scheme.

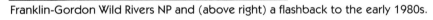

Franklin-Gordon Wild Rivers NP and (above right) a flashback to the early 1980s.

ONCE A HELL-HOLE

Port Arthur prison, on the Tasman Peninsula, was a much-feared place of suffering for convicts who re-offended after reaching Tasmania. Visitors to the peninsula today can tour its ruins and shudder at the graves on the Isle of the Dead. Other peninsula attractions are Tasmans Arch, the awesome chasm of the Devils Kitchen, the Blowholes, Doo Town and the Tessellated Pavement.

Port Arthur prison was built by convicts of rock they mined and cut into blocks by hand.

FACTS

▶ Sir Edmund Hillary, the New Zealander who conquered Mt Everest, described the Hartz Mts NP as "some of the wildest and most spectacular scenery I have ever seen".

▶ The Huon Pine is found only in SW Tas. The oldest living Huon Pine that has been dated (chopped down before Lake Pedder was flooded) was about 2500 years old. Logs 10 000 years old have been found preserved under water.

▶ Bushwalkers in Tasmania must beware of the "horizontal", a tree whose slender trunks fall over and then produce new upright trunks. In time the forest becomes a dense, matted tangle impossible to get through.

The Tessellated Pavement on the Tasman Peninsula coast.

A rich and fertile island

The northern part of Tasmania has rugged ᴳglacier-carved mountains, thick rainforests, a beautiful coastline and plenty of farming land.

The island's central west coast is an area rich in minerals. Efforts are being made to control pollution from mining operations and to restore affected country. Tasmania's eastern coast is called the Sun Coast, and is a great place for ᴳscuba diving, surfing, fishing and enjoying seaside holidays.

Alexandra Suspension Bridge crosses the South Esk River, which then flows into the Tamar.

Making a moonscape

The hills around Queenstown, on Tasmania's west coast, lost most of their vegetation because of chopping down trees to burn in the copper ᴳsmelters, the effects of sulphur fumes, and fire and reduced rainfall following ᴳdeforestation.

Eroded landscape near Queenstown.

Ice-carved wilderness

The barren mountains and high lakes of Tasmania's west were carved from the rock by ice in past ages when the world was colder.

Cradle Mtn-Lake St Clair NP is one of the most spectacular ice-created landscapes. Lake St Clair is Australia's deepest lake, at 200 m. It is the source of the Derwent, Tasmania's longest river.

Cradle Mountain, in Cradle Mtn-Lake St Clair NP, was named after either a miner's dirt-washing cradle or a baby's cradle.

40

Tasmania's Sun Coast

Tasmania's east coast is much drier and sunnier than the west coast.

Maria Island was once home to Aboriginal people, who were displaced by convicts, whalers and farmers. Today it is a national park, where wildlife which was killed out by Europeans has been reintroduced.

The holiday town of Bicheno was once known as Waubs Bay Harbour, after an Aboriginal woman, Waubedebar, who was enslaved by sealers in the early 1800s. She swam a kilometre out to sea to rescue two wrecked sealers.

The Thylacine's last refuge?

The north-western part of Tasmania has high rainfall. Along the Bass Strait coast there is fertile soil, weathered from volcanic rock. Beneath the north-western coastal plains is a network of caves dissolved by groundwater from ancient limestone rocks.

The last Thylacine, or Tasmanian Tiger, killed in the wild was shot near Mawbanna in 1930. Some people think the ᴳmarsupial may still survive around the headwaters of the Arthur River but so far there is no proof.

Pandani, or tree heath, may grow over 9 m high.

THE VANISHED THYLACINE

The Tasmanian Devil would have eaten scraps from Thylacine kills.

Bennett's Wallaby would have been the Thylacine's prey.

The Thylacine disappeared from the mainland after the Dingo, a stronger ᴳpredator, arrived. In Tasmania, it was trapped and shot. By 1936, when it was declared a protected species, it was probably extinct.

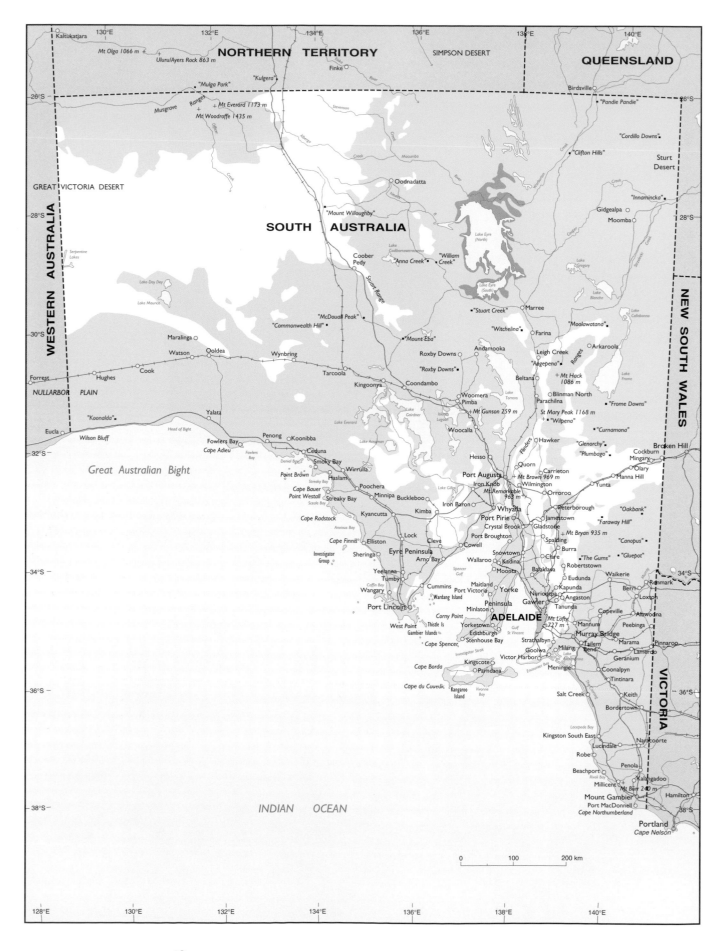

ADELAIDE (south-east coast)

	Jan	Apr	Jul	Oct
max °C	29	22	15	21
min °C	17	13	8	11
rainfall mm	20	44	67	44
rainy days	4	9	16	11

WILPENA (central north)

	Jan	Apr	Jul	Oct
max °C	31	24	13	24
min °C	16	9	3	9
rainfall mm	34	19	67	35
rainy days	3	3	9	6

State of the arts and deserts

South Australia is the driest State in Australia: over 60% is desert, and about 80% receives less than 250 mm of rain each year. The south-east corner has warm, dry summers and cool, wet winters. It has fertile soil and rich ocean resources and is the home of most of the State's population. The capital, Adelaide is noted for its promotion of the arts and is home to a famous cultural festival. Further north are ᶜmarginal lands, the Flinders Ranges and Lake Eyre. The north-east, centre and west are aridlands, noted for minerals such as opals, copper and uranium.

The Coat of Arms of SA shows the piping shrike (White Backed Magpie) set against a golden sun on a blue central shield. The grassy mound underneath has symbols of the State's prosperity: ripening wheat and

The flag of South Australia.

barley, fresh fruit, the metal cogs of industry and a miner's pick. The crest above the shield has four sprigs of the State's floral emblem, Sturt's Desert Pea, on a wreath of gold, red and blue. The motto is simply "South Australia".

KNOW MORE ABOUT SOUTH AUSTRALIA

Area: 984 000 km²
Length of coast: 3700 km
Population: 1 473 800
Driest region: Lake Eyre (about 100 mm per year)

Australia's lowest point: Lake Eyre (15 m below sea level)
Hottest recorded: 50.7°C at Oodnadatta on 2.1.1960

SA tourist attractions: Adelaide Hills; the Barossa; the Coorong; Kangaroo Is; Victor Harbor; Flinders Ra.; Whalers Way; Coober Pedy

Emblems: Floral – Sturt's Desert Pea; **Faunal** – Hairy-nosed Wombat
Badge: White Backed Magpie
Gemstone: Opal

Admirals Arch, Kangaroo Island.

Welcome to Oodnadatta.

Sturt's Stony Desert, NE of SA.

Sturt's Desert Pea.

DID YOU KNOW?

FACTS

▶ Adelaide's hottest day on record was 12.1.1939 (47.6°C). The coldest day was 24.6.1944 (ground temperature –6.1°C). The wettest day was 7.2.1925, when 141 mm of rain fell.

▶ The population of Adelaide is 1 081 000. This is 73% of the total population of SA.

▶ The three rivers which supply Adelaide are the Murray, Torrens and Onkaparinga. The fountain celebrating them is by John Dowie.

▶ A statue of William Light (*right*) stands on Montefiore Hill, overlooking the city he planned.

A city of celebrations

Adelaide stands on Gulf St Vincent, to the west of the Mt Lofty Ranges. It is a gracious city whose streets are laid out in a grid around five open squares and whose city centre is surrounded by parklands and sports fields.

Settlers arrived in SA in July 1836. Governor Hindmarsh arrived in HMS *Buffalo* and proclaimed the province of SA in December 1836. The city of Adelaide was planned by SA's first Surveyor-General, Colonel William Light.

Torrens Lake and the Festival Centre.

John Dowie's fountain in Victoria Square.

Torrens Lake

Torrens Lake was formed by building weirs to hold up the flow of the River Torrens. The lake can be explored on a Pop-Eye cruise vessel or by pedal boat.

Squares to spare

Adelaide city lies around a square of squares (Light, Whitmore, Hindmarsh and Hurtle) with Victoria Square in the centre. North Adelaide extends around Wellington Square.

1 Elder Park	**9** King Wm St, Nth Tce Intersection
2 University of Adelaide	**10** Parliament House
3 Parklands	**11** Adelaide Casino, Railway Stn
4 Art Gallery, Museum	**12** Convention Centre
5 Government House	**13** Exhibition Centre
6 Festival Centre	**14** Adelaide Hills
7 Torrens Lake	**15** Victoria Square
8 Victoria Pk Racecourse	**16** Montefiore Rd
	17 Railway Yards

44

▲ RUNDLE MALL

Pedestrians-only mall. Fruit and flower stalls. Largest shopping mall in Southern Hemisphere. Buskers entertain crowds.

▲ FESTIVAL CENTRE

Opened 1977. Venue for classical, jazz and rock concerts, plays and exhibitions. Home of Adelaide Festival of Arts (Feb/Mar. of even-numbered years). Annual children's arts festival.

▼ PORT ADELAIDE

To north-west of city centre. Many restored port buildings. Site of Maritime, Aviation and Port Dock Station Railway Museums.

▼ GLENELG BEACH

Tram ride from Victoria Square. White sandy beach. Jetty Rd lined with cafes and restaurants. Replica of HMS *Buffalo* moored nearby.

ALONG NORTH TERRACE

1 Convention Centre
2 Casino & Railway Stn
3 Festival Centre
4 Parliament House
5 Government House
6 SA Museum
7 Art Gallery of SA
8 University of Adelaide
9 University of SA
10 Royal Ad. Hospital
11 Botanic Gardens
12 Zoological Gardens

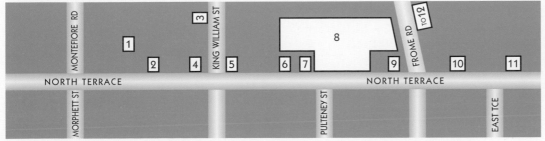

Many of Adelaide's grandest buildings and most popular attractions are near North Terrace.

At the SA Museum.

Vineyards and deserts

The south-eastern corner of SA has a climate like that of Mediterranean lands such as Spain, Italy or Greece. Hot, dry summers are followed by cool winters during which most of the year's rain falls.

The crops which grow in Mediterranean lands do well in this part of SA. Grapevines, citrus and stone fruit, almonds and wheat are grown, while sheep are kept for wool and meat.

Further north in the State, rainfall diminishes rapidly and early attempts to push farming into drier country usually failed.

Grape vines in a SA vineyard.

FROM *ZEBRA* TO HAHNDORF

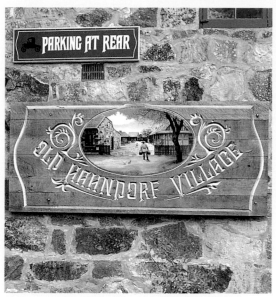

Hahndorf celebrates the town's German heritage.

Hoping for freedom to practise the Lutheran religion, German and Silesian families came to SA on the Zebra in 1839. The captain of the ship, Dirk Hahn, helped them obtain land, and they named their village after him, Hahndorf (meaning Hahn's town). Today Hahndorf pays tribute to its heritage by keeping old buildings and many customs as they were in the nineteenth century. It celebrates several German festivals.

The Fleurieu Peninsula

The Fleurieu Peninsula forms the eastern arm of Gulf St Vincent.

Once, the peninsula was used as a base by whalers. Today it is famous for wineries, especially the Southern Vales, almond orchards and plenty of places to eat. A festival called the Continuous Picnic is held each October, just before the Wine Bushing Festival. The festival called From the Sea and the Vines is held in May as a showcase for the district's produce. Port Elliot on the Peninsula's south coast is a base for surfers, sailboarders and beachsurfers (*left*).

A horse-drawn tram takes visitors from Victor Harbor to Granite Island.

DID YOU KNOW?

FACTS

▶ The wettest region of SA is around Mt Lofty, east of Adelaide, which has 1200 mm of rain each year.

▶ SA festivals include the Adelaide Festival of Arts, Womadelaide (world music) and Schutzenfest (German). The Yorke Peninsula holds Kernewek Lowender (Cornish), Port Lincoln has Tunarama, Kingston SE has Lobsterfest and Tanunda has its Oompah Festival. Mt Compass runs the famous Compass Cup, a race for cows.

Sailboarding at Waitpinga Beach.

▶ Southern Right Whales were once hunted from Victor Harbor. Now the port is the home of the SA Whale Centre, which tells visitors all about whales and where to see them swimming past.

46

Mt Gambier's Blue Lake lies in the crater of an extinct volcano. Intensely blue from November to February, it is 4.8 km around.

The south-east corner

The Murray River flows across the border with Victoria, through the fertile Riverland and enters the sea through Lake Alexandrina.

Nearby is the wild Coorong, where a continuous sandbar separates coastal lakes from the sea.

The most recent eruption by an Australian volcano was at Mt Gambier, more than 1400 years ago.

THE FLINDERS RANGES

The rocks of the Flinders Ranges, 460 km north of Adelaide, are between 1500 and 500 million years old. The rugged ranges are famous for scenic places such as Wilpena Pound (above) and for their wildlife. The rare Yellow-footed Rock-wallaby (inset) lives on steep, rocky hillsides.

A mighty salty sea

Lake Eyre, in SA's north-east, is the world's largest salt lake.

Three or four times each century it fills with water carried into it by rivers which drain over 1 million km² of the inland. It covers 9 300 km² and may reach 6 m deep. Huge flocks of birds such as pelicans fly in and breed. Unless more rain falls in the lake's catchment area, within two years the water will all have ᴳevaporated.

Races at William Creek, SA's smallest town, on Anna Creek Station near Lake Eyre.

FACTS

▶ Near Naracoorte, in the south-east, caves contain large numbers of ᴳfossilised bones of native animals.

▶ Early settlers called Blue Lake "the Devil's Inkbottle".

▶ "Wilpena" is an Aboriginal word meaning "bent fingers of a cupped hand".

▶ Adult Yellow-footed Rock-Wallabies may carry water to their young ones in their mouths.

▶ Hans Heysen was a famous SA landscape artist. The Heysen Trail stretches 1000 km from Cape Jervis north to the Flinders Ranges.

▶ At Lake Eyre, 150 mm of rain may fall in one year, but 3500 mm of water will evaporate.

▶ In 1964 Sir Donald Campbell set a world land-speed record of 645 kph on Lake Eyre, racing his jet-powered car *Bluebird* across the hardened salt crust.

▶ Australia's largest rural property, Anna Creek Station, near Lake Eyre, is half the size of Tasmania.

Island, aridland and treeless plain

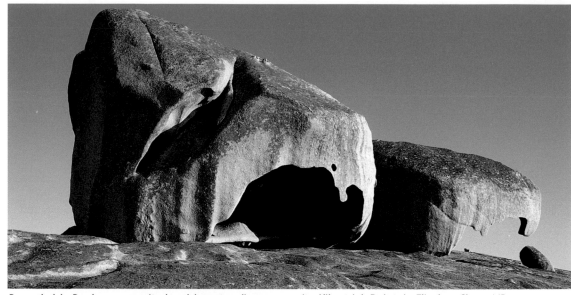

Remarkable Rocks are granite boulders standing on granite Kilpatrick Point, in Flinders Chase NP.

Australian Sea-lions can be seen at Seal Bay.

Kangaroo Island

Kangaroo Island, 120 km south-west of Adelaide, can be reached by ferry from Cape Jervis or by plane.

It is a sanctuary for wildlife, as it has no foxes, rabbits or Dingos. Things to see on the island include Remarkable Rocks, Admirals Arch, Kelly Hill Caves, Seal Bay, Koalas and colonies of Little Penguins.

CENTRAL AND NORTHERN SOUTH AUSTRALIA

Only 1% of South Australians live in the 80% of the State from Port Augusta north to the NT and Qld borders. The country is dry and hot – explorer Charles Sturt recorded 57.2ºC at Cooper Creek in 1845. Some sheep and cattle are grazed. Copper and uranium are mined, and most of the world's opals are mined at Coober Pedy and Andamooka. Much of the west is under Aboriginal control, while the Woomera rocket-launching facility is off-limits to the public.

Opal miners at work.

The WWII corvette *Whyalla* was built at Whyalla in 1941. It is now in Whyalla's Maritime Museum.

WHYALLA

The second largest SA city, Whyalla was a shipbuilding port until 1978. It now produces raw steel and pellets from ore mined at Iron Knob, Iron Monarch, Iron Duke and Iron Princess.

Next 88 km

Cliffs along the Bight.   Hazards on the Nullarbor.

THE GREAT AUSTRALIAN BIGHT

The Bight stretches for 1100 km, from Cape Carnot, SA, to Cape Pasley in WA. It is bordered by Australia's longest sea cliffs.

Saltbush grows on the plain of no trees.

THE NULLARBOR PLAIN

This "no tree" plain was pushed up from under an ancient sea by earth movements. About 750 km east to west and extending 400 km inland, it is larger than Victoria.

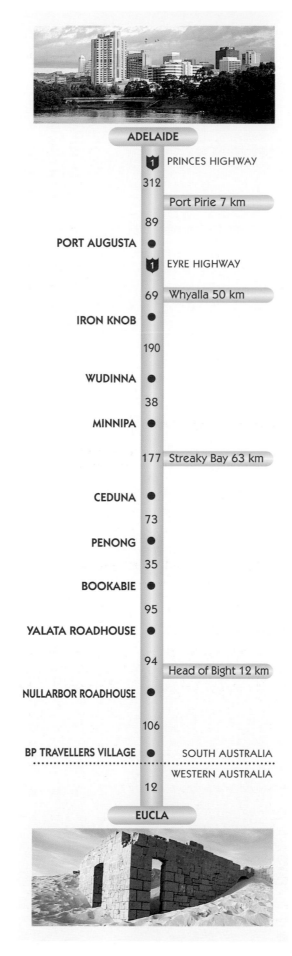

ADELAIDE

1 PRINCES HIGHWAY
312
Port Pirie 7 km
89
PORT AUGUSTA ●
1 EYRE HIGHWAY
69   Whyalla 50 km
IRON KNOB ●
190
WUDINNA ●
38
MINNIPA ●
177   Streaky Bay 63 km
CEDUNA ●
73
PENONG ●
35
BOOKABIE ●
95
YALATA ROADHOUSE ●
94   Head of Bight 12 km
NULLARBOR ROADHOUSE ●
106
BP TRAVELLERS VILLAGE ●   SOUTH AUSTRALIA
·   WESTERN AUSTRALIA
12

EUCLA

FACTS

▸ Sea cliffs at the edge of the Nullarbor Plain may reach 120 m in height.

▸ Up to 30 Southern Right Whale calves are born at Head of Bight between June and October. Head of Bight is Aboriginal land and a permit is needed to visit the cliffs there.

▸ The Nullarbor is the world's largest flat limestone surface. A vast system of caves runs under the Plain. As the caves heat and cool, air roars in and out of around 10 000 blowholes. Aboriginal legend said this was the breathing of a giant serpent.

▸ Aboriginal ᴳpetroglyphs more than 20 000 years old can be seen in Koonalda Cave on the Nullarbor.

▸ A mummified Thylacine which died 4600 years ago was found in a Nullarbor cave now named Thylacine Hole.

Looking out from inside a Nullarbor blowhole.

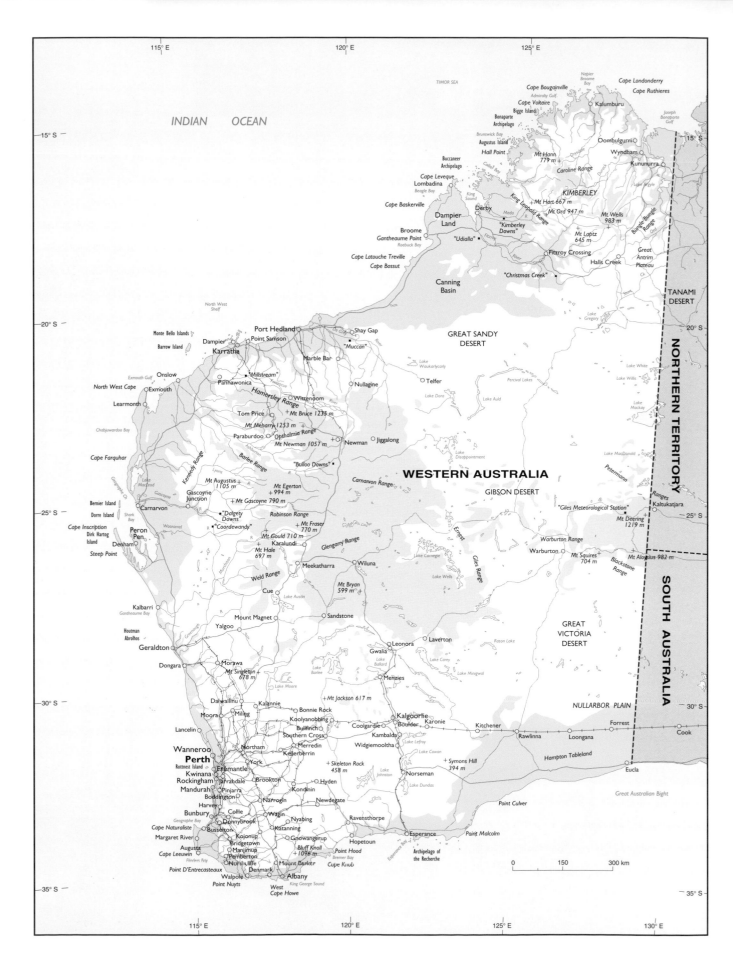

INDIAN OCEAN

TIMOR SEA

Cape Bougainville
Napier Broome Bay
Cape Londonderry
Cape Ruthieres
Admiralty Gulf.
Cape Voltaire
Kalumburu
Bigge Island
Bonaparte Archipelago
Joseph Bonaparte Gulf
Brunswick Bay
Augustus Island
Hall Point
Mt Hann 779 m +
Oombulgurri
Wyndham
Kununurra
Buccaneer Archipelago
Caroline Range
Lake Argyle
Cape Leveque
Lombadina
Beagle Bay
KIMBERLEY
Cape Baskerville
King Sound
Derby
Meda
Mt Hart 667 m +
King Leopold Range
Mt Ord 947 m
Mt Wells 983 m
Bungle Bungle Range
Dampier Land
"Kimberley Downs"
Mt Laptz 645 m +
Broome
Gantheaume Point
Roebuck Bay
"Udialla"
Fitzroy Crossing
Halls Creek
Great Antrim Plateau
Cape Latouche Treville
Cape Bossut
"Christmas Creek"

Canning Basin

TANAMI DESERT

GREAT SANDY DESERT

Lake Waukarlycarly
Lake White
Lake Wills
North West Shelf
Lake Gregory

NORTHERN TERRITORY

Monte Bello Islands
Barrow Island
Dampier
Point Samson
Port Hedland
Shay Gap
"Muccan"
Karratha
Marble Bar
Exmouth Gulf
Onslow
"Millstream"
Nullagine
Telfer
Lake Dora
Lake Auld
Lake Mackay
North West Cape
Exmouth
Pannawonica
Hamersley Range
Wittenoom
Learmonth
Tom Price
Mt Bruce 1235 m +
Lake Disappointment
Lake MacDonald
Chabjuwardoo Bay
Mt Meharry 1253 m +
Paraburdoo
Opthalmia Range
Newman
Jiggalong
Mt Newman 1057 m +
Cape Farquhar
Barlee Range
"Bulloo Downs"
WESTERN AUSTRALIA
Petermann Ranges
Kaltukatjara
Kennedy Range
Carnarvon Range
GIBSON DESERT
Mt Augustus 1105 m +
Mt Egerton 994 m +
Lake MacLeod
Bernier Island
Dorre Island
Gascoyne Junction
+ Mt Gascoyne 790 m
"Giles Meteorological Station"
Mt Deering 1219 m
Carnarvon
Robinson Range
"Dalgety Downs"
Cape Inscription
Dirk Hartog Island
Peron Pen.
"Coordewandy"
Mt Fraser 770 m +
Glengarry Range
Warburton Range
Denham
Shark Bay
Mt Gould 710 m +
Karalundi
Warburton
Mt Squires 704 m
Blackstone Range
+ Mt Aloysius 982 m
Steep Point
Mt Hale 697 m +
Meekatharra
Wiluna
Ernest
Giles Range
Lake Carnegie
Weld Range
Lake Wells
Mt Bryan 599 m +
Cue
Lake Austin
Sandstone
GREAT VICTORIA DESERT
Kalbarri
Gantheaume Bay
Mount Magnet
Yalgoo
Leonora
Laverton
Raton Lake
Houtman Abrolhos
Geraldton
Lake Ballard
Gwalia
Lake Carey
Lake Minigwal
Dongara
Morawa
Mt Singleton 678 m +
Lake Barlee
Menzies
Lake Moore
SOUTH AUSTRALIA
Dalwallinu
Kalannie
+ Mt Jackson 617 m
NULLARBOR PLAIN
Moora
Miling
Bonnie Rock
Koolyanobbing
Coolgardie
Kalgoorlie
Karonie
Kitchener
Forrest
Cook
Lancelin
Bullfinch
Boulder
Kambalda
Rawlinna
Loongana
Wanneroo
Northam
Merredin
Southern Cross
Widgiemooltha
Lake Lefroy
Perth
York
Kellerberrin
Lake Cowan
Hampton Tableland
Rottnest Island
Fremantle
Brookton
+ Skeleton Rock 458 m
+ Symons Hill 394 m
Eucla
Kwinana
Rockingham
Jarrahdale
Kondinin
Hyden
Norseman
Lake Johnston
Mandurah
Pinjarra
Lake Dundas
Boddington
Narrogin
Newdegate
Great Australian Bight
Harvey
Collie
Wagin
Point Culver
Bunbury
Donnybrook
Nyabing
Ravensthorpe
Cape Naturaliste
Katanning
Point Malcolm
Margaret River
Busselton
Kojonup
Gnowangerup
Esperance
Augusta
Bridgetown
Bluff Knoll +1096 m
Hopetoun
Cape Leeuwin
Manjimup
Point Hood
Bremer Bay
Archipelago of the Recherche
Pemberton
Mount Barker
Cape Knob
Point D'Entrecasteaux
Northcliffe
Denmark
Walpole
Albany
Point Nuyts
West Cape Howe
King George Sound
Geographe Bay
Flinders Bay
Esperance Bay

0   150   300 km

35° S
30° S
25° S
20° S
15° S

115° E   120° E   125° E   130° E

50

The mightiest State

Western Australia is the largest State of the Commonwealth. More than 90% of its surface consists of a huge plateau, whose surface is between 300 and 450 m above sea-level. In many places it drops to the sea in cliffs. The south-western corner of the State has warm dry summers and cool, rainy winters. Further north and east it rapidly becomes drier and most of the inland is desert. The discovery of minerals such as gold and iron ore has led to settlement in these remote areas. The Kimberley summer is hot and rainy and winter is warm and dry.

The coat of arms of Western Australia has two Red Kangaroos, each holding a boomerang, supporting a central shield. This shows a Black Swan on a base of rippled blue, with a silver line representing water. Above the shield is a Royal Crown on a black and gold wreath, between two kangaroo paw flowers.

PERTH (south-west coast)

	Jan	Apr	Jul	Oct
max °C	30	25	18	22
min °C	18	14	9	12
rainfall mm	8	45	173	54
rainy days	3	8	18	11

KALGOORLIE (Goldfields)

	Jan	Apr	Jul	Oct
max °C	34	25	17	26
min °C	18	12	5	11
rainfall mm	22	19	26	16
rainy days	3	5	9	4

DERBY (Kimberley)

	Jan	Apr	Jul	Oct
max °C	36	35	30	36
min °C	26	22	14	23
rainfall mm	182	32	6	2
rainy days	12	2	1	0

The flag of Western Australia.

KNOW MORE ABOUT WESTERN AUSTRALIA

Area: 2 525 500 km², 32.87% of Aust's area
Coastline length: 12 500 km
Population: 1 731 800
Most southerly point: West Cape Howe (35°08'S)

Most northerly point: Cape Londonderry (13°34'S)
Largest rock in Australia: Mt Augustus (8 km long, 3 km wide, 377 m high)

Hottest recorded in WA: 50.7°C at Eucla, 22.1.1906
Hottest place in Australia: Marble Bar, WA (summer average 41°C; above 37.8°C on 161 consecutive days)

Longest river: Gascoyne (820km)
Floral emblem: Mangles' Kangaroo Paw
Faunal emblems: Numbat and Black Swan

Coast in Torndirrup NP.

Mt Augustus.

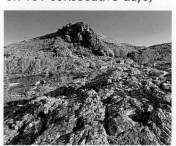

Marble Bar country.

Mangles' Kangaroo Paw.

Cities on the Swan

DID YOU KNOW?

FACTS

▶ Perth is Australia's windiest city (average wind speed 15.6 kph).

▶ Perth's hottest recorded temperature was 45.8°C on 31.1.1991. The lowest ground temperature was -3.9°C on 31.5.1964.

▶ Perth is home to 1 262 600 people (72.9% of WA's total).

▶ It is 2691 km from Perth to Adelaide via the Eyre Hwy; 4189 km to Darwin via the NW Coastal Hwy.

A jet-skier on the Swan R.

Perth city, seen across the Swan River and the Narrows Bridge.

Dutch ᶢnavigators sailing too far south and east on their way to the East Indies were the first Europeans to sight WA.

The British ᶢcolonised the Swan River in 1829. Gold, iron ore and nickel have added to the wealth brought into the State by wheat, wool and other rural products. Perth and the nearby port of Fremantle are great places to live or to visit, close to some of the world's great beaches and with the Swan River as an all-weather playground. Just inland, the Darling Range is the edge of the vast western plateau.

Cottesloe, one of Perth's magnificent beaches. Inset: A surf lifesaver at Cottesloe.

1 Parliament House	11 Government House
2 Hay St	12 Supreme Court
3 Entertainment Centre	13 The Esplanade
4 Northbridge	14 Burswood Casino
5 Railway Station	15 WA Cricket Ground
6 WA Art Gallery	16 The Causeway
7 Barracks Arch	17 Swan River
8 St Georges Tce	18 Barrack St Jetty
9 Hay St Mall	19 Narrows Interchange
10 City Busport	

▲ LONDON COURT

ᴳMock-Elizabethan street running from Hay St Mall to St Georges Tce. ᴳJousting knight clock figures (*above*). Many boutique shops.

▼ KINGS PARK

Covers 4 km² on Mt Eliza overlooking Perth and the Swan. Bushland, playgrounds, parklands, restaurant. 17 ha botanical gardens.

A port with culture

Fremantle, at the mouth of the Swan River, is home to 25 000 people and is a busy working port. It is also a place where holiday-makers mix with artists and craftspeople. Its restaurants and street cafes are usually crowded. Many people who live in "Freo" ᴳcommute 19 km to Perth to work each day.

Fremantle, seen over Success Harbour and the Fishing Boat Harbour. Fremantle Harbour is top left.

See Australia's oldest shipwrecks at the Western Australian Maritime Museum

Opening Hours
Daily: 10.30am – 5.00pm
Anzac Day & Boxing Day 1.00 pm – 5.00 pm

A shipyard at Fremantle's Maritime Museum has built a replica of the *Duyfken*, 1616 visitor to Australia.

RATS-NEST ISLAND

Quokkas are leaf-eaters.

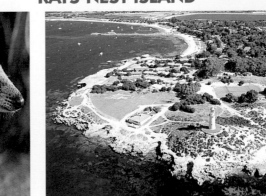

Lighthouse and Thompsons Bay, Rottnest Island.

The 19 km from Fremantle to the holiday island of Rottnest, is easily travelled in 20 minutes by fast ferry. Visitors ride bicycles on the island. It was named by Dutch captain de Vlamingh in 1696 after the wallaby-like Quokkas, which he thought were giant rats.

This craft has underwater windows.

FACTS

▶ Western Australia is famous for its wildflowers. Most of them grow best in sandy or gravelly soil and do not need lots of water. They feature in Perth's gardens and cut flowers are a big export industry.

▶ From 1838 to 1903, in a very sad piece of WA history, Rottnest was used as a prison for Aborigines. To save money, on Sundays the prisoners had to find their own food. They hunted Quokkas.

53

Australia's south-west

FACTS

▶ The Bibbulmun Walking Track begins in Kalamunda, near Perth, and ends 650 km to the south, at Walpole. The route is marked with symbols representing the Bibbulmun people's spirit-serpent, Waugal.

▶ The Valley of the Giants, where huge eucalypt trees still remain, has an annual rainfall of 1200 mm.

▶ The Karri tree can grow to more than 80 m. It is the world's third-tallest tree (after the Californian Redwood and the Australian Mountain Ash).

A surfboard rider at Yallingup.

Sugarloaf Rock, near Cape Naturaliste, is a nesting place for rare seabirds.

The south-west corner of WA is the only part of the State with regular winter rain. Carried on the westerly winds, most falls near the coast.

The extreme south-west has stands of tall trees such as Karri and Tingle and bright spring wildflowers.

Vineyards and orchards

Grapes, citrus and stone fruit, apples and pears do well in the south-west.

Margaret River, about 280 km south of Perth, is famous for quality wines, its artists and its great surf.

In some places in the south-west the soil lacks minerals which are needed for crops and animals to thrive. Farmers add minerals and fertiliser which helps enrich the soil. Native plants grow better on the original, poorer soils.

Huge Red Tingle trees in the Valley of the Giants.

Land of the giants

The Valley of the Giants, near Walpole-Nornalup NP, is a stand of giant Karri and Red Tingle trees.

It is the only place in the world where four rare species of eucalypt grow within 4 km of each other.

A beach in William Bay NP, between the towns of Walpole and Denmark.

Karri tree — one of the Four Aces, Manjimup 80 m

Red Tingle in valley of the Giants 46 m

Human 2 m tall

ONCE WERE WHALERS

Until 1978, Southern Right Whales were killed by whaling vessels based at Frenchman Bay, near Albany. Today a visit to the Whaleworld Museum 21 km from Albany can be combined with a trip to the awesome granite cliffs and silver-sand beaches in Torndirrup NP. The sights include The Gap and Natural Bridge, the Blowholes and the surfers' paradise of the Salmon Holes.

The Salmon Holes is popular with surfers.

Torndirrup NP offers challenges for rock-climbers such as The Gap (*left*) and Natural Bridge (*above*).

The wild south coast

The south coast of WA is one of the world's most scenically beautiful and unspoiled areas.

Besides the rugged Porongurup and Stirling Ranges, there are national parks at Cape Le Grand, Cape Arid and Fitzgerald River (which is a UNESCO ᴳWorld Biosphere Reserve). They are famous for wildflowers, beaches and bushwalks.

Grass-tree, Stirling Ranges.

Two Peoples Bay.

Cape Arid NP is at the western end of the Great Australian Bight, on the edge of the Nullarbor Plain.

North to adventure

North of Perth, farming land becomes sandy coastline. Towns on the coast are either fishing resorts or stand on river mouths where fresh water is available.

Cervantes, 257 km north of Perth, is the nearest town to Nambung NP. Here, the Pinnacles, pale limestone pillars up to 5 m tall, rise from a coastal sand plain. Another group of darker pillars, the Tombstones, stands nearby. They are coloured by lichen because vegetation around their bases protects them from being blasted clean by wind-blown sand.

Sand has blasted the Pinnacles into weird shapes.

The view through Nature's Window, on the lower reaches of the Murchison River. *Inset:* The size of Nature's Window is shown by the figure in front of it.

Islands of angry ghosts

Houtman Abrolhos, a group of islands offshore from Geraldton, was the scene of a shipwreck and mutiny.

In 1629, the *Batavia* was wrecked here. Most of the survivors waited on an island while Captain Pelsaert and some crew members rowed to Batavia for help. Mutineers murdered more than 120 before a rescue party arrived. Most of the renegades were tortured and hanged: two were ᴳmarooned.

Zuytdorp Cliffs, north of Kalbarri, were named after a Dutch ship wrecked offshore in 1712.

BAY OF SHARKS

Shark Bay World Heritage Area and Marine Park is home to dugong, dolphins, turtles and other threatened marine creatures.

Feeding Bottle-nosed Dolphins (*right*) at Monkey Mia.

Some pools at Shark Bay are almost land locked. Salt mining is still allowed in some places in this area of high evaporation.

Stromatolites are rocky mounds built up by layers of microscopic bacteria. Some are thousands of years old.

The Goldfields

Beyond the Wheatbelt lies the desert, where gold mining towns such as Coolgardie, Kalgoorlie-Boulder and Norseman were founded in the rushes of the 1890s.

Nickel mining and new methods of gold extraction keep these towns afloat. Wildflowers and ghost towns bring visitors to the Goldfields in the cooler winter and spring.

Wave Rock, near Hyden 350 km south-east of Perth, is a "wave" of granite 15 m high and 100 m long.

The Wheatbelt

The Wheatbelt stretches from just north of Albany to the Great Eastern Highway, and from just east of Perth to Southern Cross.

Wheat and sheep are farmed here and the best-known natural landmarks are rock formations, such as Wave Rock near Hyden.

Kalgoorlie has wide streets and many hotels.

FACTS

▶ The bacteria which form stromatolites first appeared on earth over 3.5 billion years ago. The stromatolites are one reason Shark Bay is listed as a World Heritage area.

▶ The bands of darker colour on Wave Rock are caused by the run-off of rainwater carrying minerals.

▶ The biggest hailstone recorded in Australia (15 x 7.5 cm) crashed through a tent at Bullfinch, just north of Southern Cross, on 13.4.1918.

▶ Dryandra State Forest, in the southern Wheatbelt, is a refuge for the endangered, termite-eating Numbat and other rare native mammals, as well as for the threatened Mallee Fowl.

The endangered Numbat.

A final frontier

The Coral Coast, which is the section of WA's coastline from north of Shark Bay to Onslow, is one of the world's best places to see marine life.

The Pilbara stretches from Onslow to north of Port Hedland and inland past the Hamersley Range. Its rocks are very ancient and it has fabulous deposits of iron ore which have led to the establishment of mining towns.

The eastern edge of the Great Sandy Desert separates the Pilbara and the Kimberley Division. It is 610 km from Port Hedland to Broome, including the dunes and shell-rich sands of Eighty Mile Beach. Broome was once a pearl-diving port, and is now a great holiday place and a gateway to the Kimberley.

The arid landscape of the Kennedy Range.

A gorge in the Hamersley Range, Karijini NP.

A record-breaking rock

The world's largest monolith, Mt Augustus, is 450 km from Carnarvon.

It is twice the size of Uluru, but has bushes covering its lower part. Its granite foundation is around 1750 million years old.

Red, hot and full of iron

Travellers in the Pilbara need to carry water, for in summer it can be one of the world's hottest places.

Winter and spring are the times to visit, to see wildflowers and the huge open-cut mines which produce iron ore.

Aboriginal legend says that Mt Augustus is the remains of a speared traveller named Burringurrah.

Ningaloo Marine Park, at North West Cape, is the place to swim with Whale Sharks, Manta Rays (left) and Humpback Whales.

Mustering in the Kimberley must be done in the Dry.

The mighty Kimberley

The West Kimberley has huge cattle stations, cultured pearl farms and rugged limestone ranges which 350 million years ago were coral reefs under an ancient sea.

The East Kimberley has cattle stations too. At Kununurra, irrigation from Lake Argyle grows tropical crops, while diamonds are mined at Argyle.

The Prince Regent Nature Reserve, in the north-western Kimberley, is a World Biosphere Reserve. Landing and camping here are prohibited. The area can be viewed only from the air or from a boat on one of the coastal rivers.

A tidal "waterfall" on the Kimberley coast.

The Boab tree's nearest relatives are in Africa and Madagascar. It sheds its leaves in the Dry.

THE DOMES OF PURNULULU

Originally known as the Bungle Bungles, the 350-million-year-old domes of Purnululu, 305 km from Kununurra, were revealed to the world by a TV crew as late as 1982. Striped by bands of silica and darker lichen, the domes are fragile and are easily damaged by climbers' boots.

The tombstone of a Japanese pearl diver in Broome cemetery.

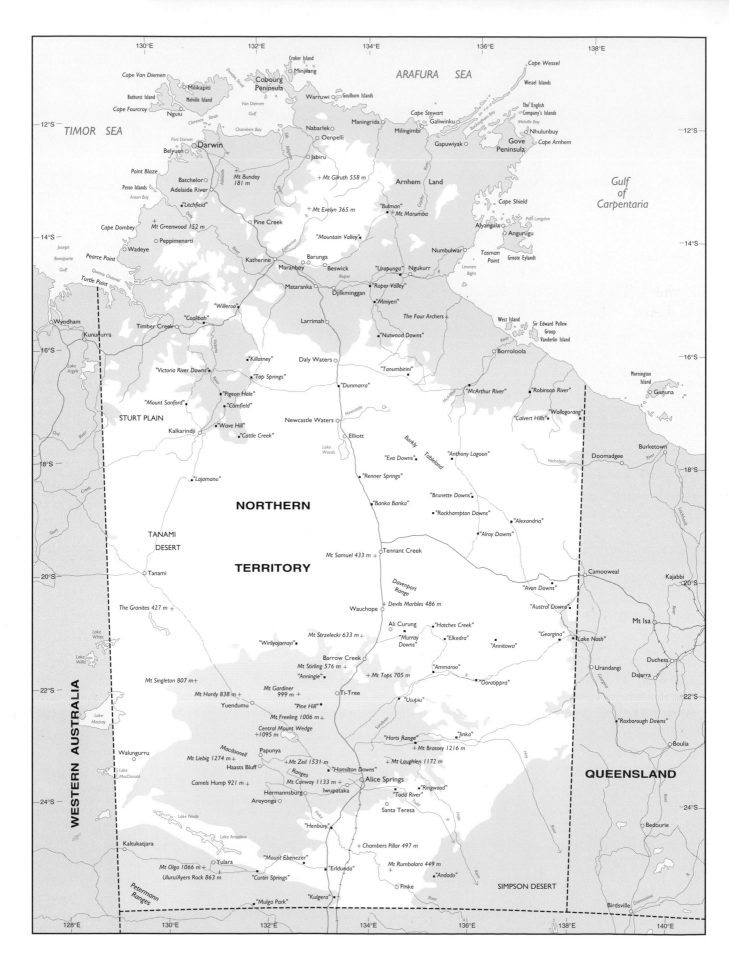

Nature Territory

The Northern Territory's coastline is washed by the Timor and Arafura Seas and the Gulf of Carpentaria. These are bordered by sandy beaches, mudflats and mangrove swamps. Southwards are coastal plains, crossed by numerous rivers, then the edge of a low tableland. This slopes up gradually towards the desert area known as the Red Centre. The main features of the Centre are rugged ranges and huge rocks rising suddenly from the desert plains.

The Coat of Arms of the Northern Territory features a shield supported by two Red Kangaroos holding shells. On the shield are a female figure, in Aboriginal x-ray art style, and two motifs representing a Churunga, a sacred map-like carving. Above the shield is a Wedge-tailed Eagle on an Aboriginal rock. Beneath the rock is a helmet. On either side of the shield is a sprig of Sturt's Desert Rose.

DARWIN (Top End)

	Jan	Apr	Jul	Oct
max °C	32	33	30	33
min °C	25	24	19	25
rainfall mm	406	97	1	74
rainy days	21	9	1	7

ALICE SPRINGS (centre)

	Jan	Apr	Jul	Oct
max °C	36	28	19	31
min °C	21	13	4	15
rainfall mm	36	14	16	21
rainy days	5	2	3	5

The flag of the Northern Territory.

KNOW MORE ABOUT THE NORTHERN TERRITORY

Total area: 1 346 200 km²
% of area of Aust: 17.52
Coastline length: 6200 km
Population: 174 100
Longest river: Victoria (650 km)

Most rain in one day: Roper Valley (545 mm on 15.4.1963)
Longest cave: Cutta Cutta Cave, south of Katherine (2000 m)

Mined: Uranium, bauxite, gold, manganese ore, copper, uranium, iron ore
Largest ᴳpredator: Saltwater Crocodile

Floral emblem: Sturt's Desert Rose
Faunal emblems: Wedge-tailed Eagle and Red Kangaroo

Northern Territory coastline.

Top End wetlands after rain.

Sturt's Desert Rose.

Wedge-tailed Eagle.

A gateway to the world

DID YOU KNOW?

FACTS

- The hottest day in Darwin reached 40.5°C on 17.11.1982. The wettest day was 7.1.1987 (296 mm of rain fell). Darwin has about 74 thunderstorms each year, but only 2 foggy days.

- On Christmas Day, 1974, Cyclone Tracy struck Darwin with wind speeds of up to 300 km/h. Sixty-six people were killed and over 30 000 were evacuated. After Tracy, the Australian Government was reluctant to rebuild Darwin in the same place. The Darwinites simply started building.

- Food and housing cost more in Darwin than anywhere else in Australia.

Darwin's dry season sunsets are spectacular. This one is seen over Fannie Bay.

Darwin was established in 1869 as a port and a centre for the cattle industry. Today the Northern Territory is increasingly important for its mineral wealth, as a major tourist attraction and as Australia's gateway to South-East Asia.

The capital of the Northern Territory has a population of around 80 000 (about 45.6% of the NT's total) and is Australia's most multicultural city. Darwin has a tropical climate, with hot, wet summers and very warm, dry winters.

Old Darwin Police Station and Courthouse (1884).

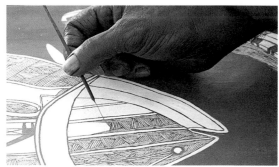

Darwin galleries specialise in Aboriginal art.

Enjoying the Variety Club Bash.

MINDIL BEACH

Although swimming at Mindil Beach is limited by stinging box jellyfish in summer, there's plenty of other fun to be had there.

Weekly markets are held in the Dry.

Is it sinking? An anxious moment at the annual Can Regatta.

PLACES TO SEE IN DARWIN

◄ THE WHARF PRECINCT

End of Stokes Hill Wharf. Open-air eating areas and plenty of different foods (great fish and chips). Families and friends gather at night to eat and party. Nearby Survivors Lookout tells story of WWII bombings.

MUSEUMS ►

NT Museum and Art Gallery at Fannie Bay. Aviation Heritage Centre near Winellie (right). Military Museum at East Point. Fannie Bay Gaol Museum. Indo-Pacific Marine, Wharf Precinct.

◄ THE ESPLANADE

Borders Port Darwin. Runs past public buildings such as Parliament House, Government House, as well as historic houses, hotels, monuments. At NW end is Doctors Gully, where fish come in to be fed at high tide (left).

FACTS

▶ Darwin has residents of more than 50 nationalities.

▶ Rules at the Can Regatta at Mindil Beach include "thou shalt not drown" and "thy craft shall float by cans alone". In the Henley-on-Mindil event, bottomless boats are raced on the beach.

▶ The Tour Tub is an open-sided bus which tours Darwin sights. A day ticket entitles the holder to get on and off as many times as they wish.

▶ Crocodiles can be seen at Crocodylus Park or Darwin Crocodile Farm.

1 Doctors Gully	**10** Ferry Terminal
2 Daly St	**11** Lyons Cottage
3 Small Boat Harbour	**12** Parliament House
4 The Esplanade	**13** Stokes Hill Wharf
5 Bicentennial Park	**14** Survivors Lookout
6 Transit Centre	**15** Wharf Precinct
7 Frances Bay	**16** Government House
8 Smith St Mall	**17** Lamaroo Beach
9 Pearling Exhibition	**18** Port Darwin

DID YOU KNOW?

Land of the monsoon

The Top End is the name often used for the northernmost part of the Northern Territory. It is a land of summer rainfall, brought by monsoons and dumped in huge quantities on the floodplains and sandstone highlands.

While the wetlands are flooded, birds, frogs, crocodiles and insects breed in great numbers. Once the rain stops, the water dries up and eventually wildlife gathers around rivers and billabongs. Many people prefer to visit the northern part of the Territory in the cooler, dry winter, when it is more comfortable and easier to travel. However they miss the excitement and the adventure of seeing the Top End when the waterfalls are flowing and wildlife is everywhere.

FACTS

▶ Northern Territorians usually refer to the seasons as the Wet and the Dry. The Buildup is the pre-Wet time of lightning storms and humid heat. Tourism promoters now talk about the "Green" rather than the "Wet".

▶ Magnetic termite mounds are built by tiny, blind insects. They are ᵍoriented so that they get least sun at the hottest time of day.

▶ At the Territory Wildlife Park, a very large Saltwater Crocodile eyeballs visitors longingly through the (thick) glass side of its swimming pool.

▶ On the Adelaide River, 67 km from Darwin, crocodiles leap from the water to grab meat held out on poles by cruise boat operators. They may lift all but their tail from the river.

Magnetic termite mounds in Litchfield NP. Their narrow edges are oriented north–south.

Florence Falls in Litchfield NP, a great place to walk, swim and play 115 km south of Darwin.

Gorgeous gorges

The town of Katherine is 335 km south of Darwin. Nitmiluk NP is 30 km east of the town.

Here, the Katherine River has carved 13 magnificent sandstone gorges, which stretch for 12 km. They are connected by stony bars and can be explored by walking, from canoes or on a cruise boat.

A Saltwater Crocodile at the Territory Wildlife Park, 60 km from Darwin.

What big teeth!

Saltwater Crocodiles live in the Territory's seas and coastal rivers. A "saltie" may grow to 6 m and will eat any animal it can catch, including human beings. Crocodiles are farmed for leather and meat, and as tourist attractions.

A leaping Saltwater Crocodile and an advertising replica (*right*).

Cruising on the Katherine. Floods can fill the spectacular gorges of Nitmiluk NP in the Wet.

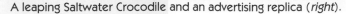

SIX SEASONS IN KAKADU

GUDJEWG (Dec-Mar)
Hot, wet ^Gmonsoon time. Thunderstorms, rain, flooding. Plants grow, birds and frogs breed.

BANGERRENG (Mar-May)
Harvest time. Storms flatten 2 m high spear grass. Plants flower and fruit, animals have young.

GUNUMELENG (Oct-Dec)
Build-up to monsoon. Heat and clouds increase, lightning, fires.

YEGGE (May-June)
Cool, dry weather. Waterlilies on swamps. Gagadju fire bush.

The Gagadju people who own and manage Kakadu divide the year into six seasons. Each season covers a different part of the weather cycle, the foods available and the people's way of life.

GURRUNG (Aug-Oct)
Hot dry season. Water and green feed scarce. Plants may shed leaves. Reptiles active.

WURRGENG (June-Aug)
Early dry season. Mammals breed. Creeks drying up.

The entrance to Kakadu National Park is 250 km east of Darwin. It covers coastal river floodplains and the sandstone Arnhem Land ^GEscarpment, and is famous for wildlife, Aboriginal rock art and spectacular scenery.

Aboriginal rock paintings in Kakadu NP.

FACTS

▶ When spear grass is flattened by storms, each seed drills into the soil as its tail shaft uncoils. When fire sweeps across the plains, the seed is safe underground.

▶ Kakadu is World Heritage listed for outstanding cultural (human) and natural (environmental) values.

▶ Uranium mining in the NT is not popular with anti-nuclear activists.

▶ Aboriginal rock paintings can be seen in many places in Kakadu NP. Usually they are in caves or under over-hanging rock. Humans have used these places for shelter for more than 40 000 years.

Aboriginal people own a number of NT cattle stations.

Red in the Centre

FACTS

▶ In July 1976 Alice Springs had a record minimum of -7.5°C.

▶ At the town's Henley-on-Todd races, bottomless boats are carried on the dry bed of the Todd River.

It is 1508 km from Darwin to Alice Springs, through country that quickly becomes more and more arid. However it has plenty of life of its own, which may only become active in the cooler evening and night. Late afternoon to dawn is the time to see wildlife in this country, but drivers need to be especially alert to avoid collisions with kangaroos, emus, cattle and ᴳferal pigs.

The Devils Marbles are right beside the Stuart Hwy. *Inset:* A "marble" being reshaped.

▶ The Devils Marbles lie beside the Stuart Highway south of Tennant Creek. They were formed 1500 million years ago as one huge granite outcrop which weathered into boulders.

▶ Traditional Aboriginal belief is that the Devil's Marbles are eggs of the Rainbow Serpent which formed the land on its journeys.

▶ At Mataranka, 110 km south of Katherine, there is a ᴳthermal pool.

Who was Alice?

In the 1870s a repeater station for the Overland Telegraph line was built at Alice Springs, on the Todd River in central Australia. Alice was the wife of SA Postmaster-General, Sir Charles Heavitree Todd, whose staff named the springs.

When the telegraph station was transferred to the nearby town of Stuart, the town was renamed.

The Old Telegraph Station, near the Alice Springs.

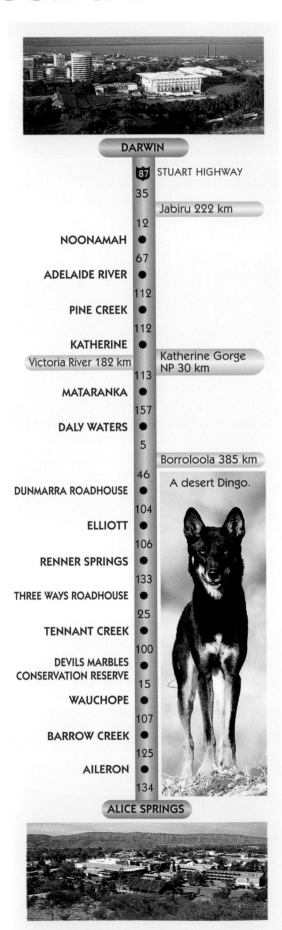

DARWIN

87 STUART HIGHWAY

35

Jabiru 222 km

12

NOONAMAH

67

ADELAIDE RIVER

112

PINE CREEK

112

KATHERINE

Victoria River 182 km — Katherine Gorge NP 30 km

113

MATARANKA

157

DALY WATERS

5

Borroloola 385 km

46

DUNMARRA ROADHOUSE

A desert Dingo.

104

ELLIOTT

106

RENNER SPRINGS

133

THREE WAYS ROADHOUSE

25

TENNANT CREEK

100

DEVILS MARBLES CONSERVATION RESERVE

15

WAUCHOPE

107

BARROW CREEK

125

AILERON

134

ALICE SPRINGS

THE MACDONNELL RANGES

The MacDonnell Ranges run in parallel ridges for about 400 km across the centre of Australia. Once rivers flowed south across them, carving gorges through the sandstone. Today the rivers are usually dry, and water can be found only in pools sheltered by rocky cliffs and kept filled by winter rains.

Simpsons Gap, carved through Rungutjirba Ridge by Roe Creek, is 22 km west of Alice Springs.

Palm Valley, cut from the James Range by the Finke River, is one of the world's oldest watercourses.

Uluru's sandstone glows in the sunrise.

The big red rock

Uluru-Kata Tjuta National Park is 470 km south-west of Alice Springs.

Uluru is a well-known symbol of Australia. This huge rock rises 348 m, and more and more of its height is visible as the sand blows away from the desert plain around it. It is 3.6 km long and 2.4 km across, and about two-thirds is still below the sand.

Kata Tjuta is just over 30 km west of Uluru. The tallest dome is nearly 200 m higher than Uluru.

Thanks, but we don't drink

Some desert animals such as Dingos must live near water.

Others, like the endangered Bilby and tiny hopping-mice, rarely drink. They obtain enough water from the seeds, roots and insects they eat.

The Bilby.

▶ The 3000 Livistona palm trees in Palm Valley are survivors from times when central Australia had areas of rainforest.

A Livistona palm tree

▶ Visitors to Uluru must sleep outside the national park, at Yulara.

▶ The Anangu people, the area's traditional guardians, prefer visitors not to climb Uluru. They call people who do climb it "ants".

▶ Kata Tjuta means "many heads".

To Aboriginal people, Chambers Pillar, 160 km south of Alice Springs, represents Itirkawara, a gecko ancestor of the Dreaming.

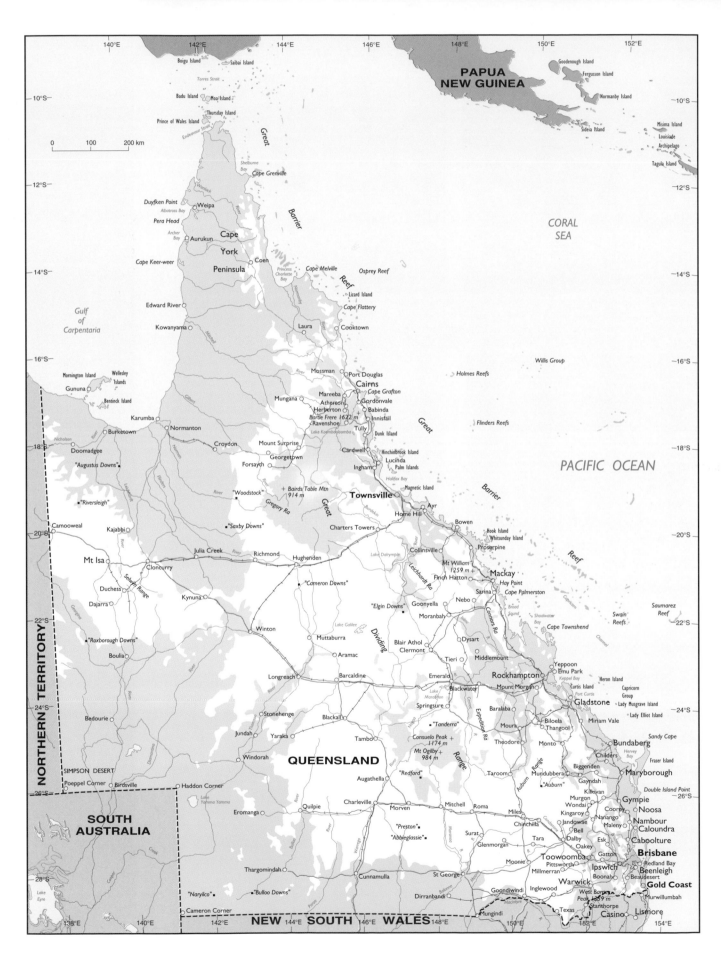

BRISBANE (south east coast)				
	Jan	Apr	Jul	Oct
max °C	29	27	21	26
min °C	21	17	10	16
rainfall mm	169	86	66	102
rainy days	14	11	7	10

CAIRNS (north-west coast)				
	Jan	Apr	Jul	Oct
max °C	31	29	26	29
min °C	24	22	17	21
rainfall mm	413	191	28	38
rainy days	18	17	9	8

A State of natural beauties

Queensland takes up about one-fifth of the area of Australia. Along its eastern coastline are fertile plains and river valleys which may extend up to 200 km inland. The Great Dividing Range borders these lowlands, stretching from Cape York south to the NSW border. In the north-west of the State are the grasslands of the Barkly Tableland. The south-west is plainland, drained by a network of rivers, which after heavy rain flood the Channel Country as they flow towards Lake Eyre.

On the Coat of Arms, a Red Deer, representing the Old World, and a Brolga, representing native-born Queenslanders, support a shield. On it are a sheaf of wheat, the heads of a bull and a ram, and a column of gold rising from a heap of ᶜquartz.

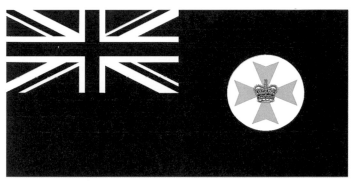

The flag of Queensland.

The badge above shows allegiance to the Queen and two stalks of sugar. The motto is Audax at Fidelis, meaning "Bold but faithful".

This Coat of Arms, granted in 1893, is the oldest in Australia.

KNOW MORE ABOUT QUEENSLAND

Area: 1 727 200 km²
Coastline length: 7400 km
Population: 3 276 700
% of indigenous people living in Qld: 26.3

Hottest place: Cloncurry (53.1°C on 16.1.1889)
Birthplace of world's second-oldest airline: Longreach (Qantas founded 1920)

Qld has three corners: it meets the NT and SA at Poeppel Corner; SA at Haddon Corner; NSW and SA at Cameron Corner

Floral emblem: Cooktown Orchid
Faunal emblems: Brolga and Koala

Snorkelling in tropical waters.

In Queensland's hottest region.

The hotel at Cameron Corner.

Cooktown Orchid.

DID YOU KNOW?

FACTS

▶ The population of Brisbane is 1 489 100, 45.7% of that of Qld.

▶ Brisbane's highest and lowest temperatures were 43.2°C on 26.1.1940 and -4.5°C on 11.7.1890.

▶ On 1.1.1969, drifts of hailstones up to 3.7 m deep killed more than 200 cows at Lowood near Brisbane. On 4.11.1973, a tornado with winds up to 253 km/h hit the city.

▶ Brisbane's South Bank Parkland was built on the site of the 1988 World Expo.

▶ The original Aboriginal inhabitants of Moreton Bay hunted fish with the help of wild dolphins, who drove prey towards their spears, traps and nets.

City on Moreton Bay

Brisbane was settled in 1825 as a prison for the worst NSW convicts.

Today it is an exciting modern city with a fast-growing population, noted for its subtropical climate and outdoor lifestyle. The Brisbane River flows into Moreton Bay and salt water may reach up to 90 km upstream.

Brisbane's City Hall was built in the 1920s.

This magnificent swimming lagoon and beach, at South Bank Parklands, is right next to the Brisbane River.

These towers behind the Riverside Centre have been called "the stockman and his blue heeler".

Places to play

Well-known Brisbane places include South Bank Parklands, the Riverside Centre, Queen Street Mall and Fortitude Valley.

Brisbane has two Botanic Gardens, one in the city and one at Mt Coot-tha. To the west is Brisbane Forest Park, which includes 28 500 ha of the Great Dividing Range.

1 City Botanic Gardens	**3** Kangaroo Point	**5** Merivale Bridge	**7** Dockside	**9** Riverside Centre	**11** Customs House	**13** New Farm
2 Qld Cultural Centre	**4** Mt Coot-tha	**6** Waterfront Place	**8** The Pier	**10** Brisbane River	**12** Captain Burke Park	**14** Story Bridge

THE GOLD COAST

The Gold Coast is just south of Brisbane and its beaches stretch about 50 km from Sanctuary Cove to Coolangatta. Attractions include beaches (top left), Sea World (top right), Dreamworld (above left) and Currumbin Sanctuary, where wild lorikeets come to be fed (above right).

There's green behind the gold

Inland from the Gold Coast is some of Australia's most exciting rainforest.

Once, a huge volcano erupted on a spur of the Great Dividing Range. Today it is extinct, but its lava flows have weathered into a tableland edged with steep cliffs and covered with rainforest. Lamington and Springbrook NPs are full of ancient beech trees, unique rainforest, waterfalls and wild creatures, some found nowhere else.

Crimson Rosella.

Chalahn Falls, Lamington NP, and (*inset*) an Australian King-Parrot.

A pair of Sugar Gliders.

71

FACTS

▶ At Currumbin Sanctuary, Rainbow and Scaly-breasted Lorikeets feast on a special mixture. Their normal food is ᴳnectar, licked from flowers with their brush-tipped tongues.

The Lamington Blue Cray is unique to the McPherson Ranges.

▶ A strangler fig begins as a tiny seed lodged on the bark of a rainforest tree. Its roots go down to the ground around its host's trunk. Eventually the host dies, leaving the fig in its place.

Strangler fig and crowsnest fern.

A coastal paradise

Looking across Pumicestone Passage from Bribie I to the mainland and the Glass House Mountains.

The beaches and coastal lakes of the Sunshine Coast are just north of Brisbane. On the way are the Glass House Mountains, named in 1770 by Captain James Cook, and the Big Pineapple, a tourist information centre about the fruit.

DID YOU KNOW?

FACTS

▶ Captain Cook named the Glass House Mountains after the glass-making furnaces of his native Yorkshire. Their Aboriginal names include Tibrogargan and Canowrin.

▶ In 1799, Matthew Flinders saw about 600 Bribie Island Aborigines living in huts 4–5 m long. The last Bribie Aborigine, Kal-ma-Kutha, died in 1897.

▶ The sand islands of Moreton Bay and Fraser Island are made of sand carried by waves and wind from the north coast of NSW.

▶ Conservationists led by John Sinclair had Fraser Island World Heritage listed, which stopped logging and sand mining there. Sinclair was ᵍbankrupted by his struggle to save the island's assets.

FRASER ISLAND

World Heritage listed Fraser Island (above), 190 km north of Brisbane, is the world's largest sand island, 120 km long and 15 km wide. It is famous for its massive sand dunes, freshwater lakes, rainforests and pure-blooded Dingos (above right). A 4-wheel-drive vehicle (right) is needed to see the full beauty of the island.

Whales watching?

Hervey Bay is the base for boats carrying people to watch Humpback Whales as they swim to their Barrier Reef breeding grounds.

Cruise boat operators are careful not to disturb the whales, but sometimes the ocean giants surface near boats and appear to be watching the watchers.

Whale-watching boats operate from late July to mid-October.

A Humpback Whale ᵍbreaching.

THE GREAT BARRIER REEF

The Great Barrier Reef stretches south from Torres Strait to just north of Fraser Island. It has about 900 islands and covers an area greater than Victoria or Great Britain. Above is Green Island, just offshore from Cairns.

The coral which makes up reefs is the hard outer skeleton which protects the soft bodies of tiny coral animals called polyps. Many sorts of polyps live in ᴳcolonies (*above*). Some corals grow towards the surface at 300 mm per year.

There are many remarkable relationships between quite different creatures which live on a coral reef. The anemone fish shown above shelters amongst the ᴳvenomous tentacles of the sea anemone.

Ways to see the Reef include reef-walking, snorkelling, scuba-diving, through glass in a boat or in an aquarium.

Raine Island

NEAREST MAINLAND TOWN	ISLAND OR GROUP OF ISLANDS
10°41'S NORTHERN LIMIT OF REEF	
LOCKHART RIVER	• Raine Island
	• Lizard Island
COOKTOWN	
PORT DOUGLAS	• Low Isles
CAIRNS	• Green Island
INNISFAIL	
	• Dunk Island
TULLY	• Bedarra Island
CARDWELL	• Hinchinbrook Island
INGHAM	• Orpheus Island
	• Palm Island
TOWNSVILLE	• Magnetic Island
	• Hayman Island
BOWEN	• Hook Island
PROSERPINE	• WHITSUNDAY GROUP
	• LINDEMAN GROUP
	• Brampton Island
MACKAY	
	• NORTHUMBERLAND GROUP
	• Townsend Island
YEPOON	• Great Keppel Island
ROCKHAMPTON	
Tropic of Capricorn	
	• Curtis Island
GLADSTONE	• CAPRICORN GROUP
	• Heron Island
	• BUNKER GROUP
	• Lady Musgrave Island
	• Lady Elliot Island
24°30'S SOUTHERN LIMIT OF REEF	
BUNDABERG	• Fraser Island
	• Bribie Island
	• Moreton Island
	• Stradbroke Island

Lady Musgrave Island and surrounding reef.

FACTS

▶ The Great Barrier Reef is the world's largest coral structure. It is made up of more than 2900 individual coral reefs.

▶ There have been coral reefs on Queensland's southern ᴳcontinental shelf for up to 2 million years, and on the northern shelf for 18 million years.

▶ When Ice Ages locked up seawater in ice caps, shallow coastal waters and coral reefs disappeared. The present Reef began to grow when melting ice caps flooded coastal plains about 10 000 years ago.

▶ The Great Barrier Reef was declared a World Heritage area in 1981.

▶ The Great Barrier Reef gets most of its rain in summer from tropical ᴳcyclones. On 24.12.1971, when Cyclone Althea struck Townsville, wind gusts reached 196 kph and 3 people died. In January 1970, Cyclone Ada caused the deaths of 13 people on the Whitsunday Coast. In March 1956, Cyclone Agnes struck Townsville and Cairns, killing 4.

Rainforest and Reef

Queensland's north-east coast is the home of two incredible natural treasures, the Great Barrier Reef and tropical rainforest.

World Heritage listed rainforest can be found in a long, narrow coastal strip between Townsville and Cooktown. This area is very important because so much of the world's rainforest has already been destroyed. Many of the plants and animals found in Australia's rainforests live nowhere else on earth.

Heading for a coral cay.

Magic islands

The Whitsunday group of continental islands lies close offshore between Bowen and Mackay.

The islands are fringed with coral reefs and seven have holiday resorts. Bareboating, or sailing the islands in a hired vessel, is a popular way to see the Whitsundays.

Capricorn Coast

The Capricorn Coast extends on either side of the Tropic of Capricorn.

Rockhampton, "beef capital of Australia", the area's major town, is just north of the Tropic. Off the coast are the southern Barrier Reef islands. Inland is the Central Highlands, a fertile farming and grazing area with vast coal deposits.

Whitehaven Beach, Whitsunday Island.

Fishing Tropical North Queensland style.

Rafting down the Tully River in the Wet.

Cairns, capital of Queensland's Tropical North.

Enjoying Agincourt Reef from a dive boat.

Skyrail travels from near Cairns over rainforest to Kuranda.

Tableland treasures

The Atherton Tableland, to the west of Cairns, has an average altitude of 762 m and covers about 32 000 km^2.

It has rich volcanic soil and two lakes, Eacham and Barrine, which were once volcanic craters.

The Tjapukai dancers can be seen at Caravonica Lakes, near Cairns.

Horse-riding along the beach at Port Douglas, 65 km north of Cairns and a high-profile holiday resort town.

WET TROPICS WORLD HERITAGE AREA

Some of the forests in the Wet Tropics area have never been logged. They are unique sanctuaries for many rare species of animals and plants.

The rare Green Python lives in tropical rainforest.

In tropical rainforest.

FACTS

▸ Bellenden Ker, just south of Cairns, received the record-breaking amount of 11 251 mm of rain during 1979.

▸ With an annual average rainfall of 4084 mm, Tully is Australia's wettest town.

▸ The rainforest which covered much of the Atherton Tableland was cleared for dairy farms.

▸ Cape York Peninsula is 700 km long. Its tip, the northernmost point of Australia, is separated by 140 km of sea from Papua New Guinea.

▸ It is 952 km from Cairns to the tip of Cape York Peninsula. In the Wet, many roads are cut by flooded rivers. Pajinka Wilderness Lodge is a few hundred metres from the very tip of the Cape. It is owned and run by the local Aboriginal people.

The tip of Cape York, Australia's northernmost mainland point.

Queensland's Outback

The Central Highlands of Queensland consist of 15 individual, deeply eroded sandstone ranges,

Carnarvon National Park, whose best-known feature is Carnarvon Gorge, is 720 km north-west of Brisbane. Carnarvon Creek has carved a ravine 30 km long and sometimes 200 m deep to create a magic world of deep pools, moss gardens, wildlife and Aboriginal art.

Possum, Carnarvon Gorge.

Viewing platforms protect rock art from harm.

Setting out to explore Carnarvon Gorge.

No fighting at mealtimes

The Bunya Mountains are 230 km north-west of Brisbane.

Before Europeans arrived, the local Aboriginal people gathered in the mountains every three years to harvest and eat the nuts of the Bunya pines. Other groups were invited to join them, and during the harvest ceremonies were held and arguments settled peacefully. After 1870, White timber-getters cut the red cedar from the mountains, then the largest pines as well. Today a national park, declared in 1908, protects more than 11 000 ha of the mountains, but the Aborigines are long gone.

Lawn Hill NP, an oasis in the tropical Gulf Savanna.

Yarding beasts on a Gulf Savanna cattle station.

The Stockmans Hall of Fame and Outback Heritage Centre at Longreach. It was the brainchild of bushman and businessman R M Williams and artist Hugh Sawrey.

The Channel Country

The corner of Queensland which borders the NT, SA and NSW, is criss-crossed by water channels.

It hardly ever rains in this area, but water from the summer monsoons

It's a long way from The Isa to almost anywhere.

Birdsville and beyond

Queensland's remotest town, Birdsville is 12 km from the SA border. In the late 1800s, it was a ᴳCustoms point for cattle being driven along the 481 km track to Marree, SA.

The Simpson Desert NP stretches across the Qld, NT and SA borders. It is hot, dry country, noted for its long, high sand dunes. Travellers should take at least two 4-wheel-drive vehicles and plenty of water and fuel, and notify police of their plans.

further north floods along Cooper Creek and the Diamantina and other rivers. Cattle are moved in to graze on the new growth of native grasses. On a few occasions each century, floodwaters reach Lake Eyre and it becomes full of breeding waterbirds.

The Isa is a survivor

Mt Isa exists because of rich copper, silver, lead and zinc ores.

Mt Isa Mines was formed in 1924. "The Isa" has the biggest silver and lead production in the Western world and is in the top 10 producers of copper and zinc. Ore is transported by rail 900 km to Townsville.

Sand dunes in the Simpson Desert.

Back up your memories

Australia is a huge land. It is easy to enjoy each day's travel but end your journey with no clear memories. If you go to faraway places and have magical adventures there, you will want to *relive the experiences time and time again. Here are some suggestions which may help you record your discoveries in words and pictures, then retrieve them when you reach home once more.*

RESEARCH AND PLAN

Treat Australia as a foreign country. Research your destination (try books, the Internet, State tourist bureau handouts, automobile club information, road maps and atlases). Know where you are going and what to look for when you get there. If some place you particularly want to see is not on the trip agenda, see if it can be included.

RECORD AS YOU GO

Take the equipment you will need to record your journey. A notebook and several pens or pencils, your own road map on which you can write and your own (or the family) camera or video. As you travel, jot notes to remind yourself of things to write up each evening. Try to set down your feelings as well as the things you are seeing.

SPOT THE DIFFERENCES

Look at the ways in which people and places are different from each other. Someone who has lived in Sydney or Hobart all their life will probably speak and act quite differently from someone born and raised in Widgiemooltha, Borroloola or Triabunna. Ask why places and people and plants and animals are the way they are. Then look for the answers.

MAKE YOUR OWN ARCHIVES

When you get home again, spend some time sorting out your notes and getting your photos developed and into albums. You could put together a newsletter (this is where a computer is ideal) and send it to friends. If you do this, don't be surprised if they get really jealous and go off on their own adventures so they can brag to you.

Glossary & Acknowledgements

Arid. Dry; without moisture.
Bacteria. Microscopic, simple lifeforms.
Bankrupted. Made unable to pay debts.
Basalt. Dark, dense rock of a lava flow.
Bicentenary. Two-hundredth birthday.
Blast furnaces. Chambers in which minerals are melted using forced draughts of air.
Blockaded. Cut off from receiving supplies.
Breaching. Of whales, leaping from the water.
Census. Official count of population.
Circumference. Distance around.
Circumnavigated. Travelled around.
Clone. Exact copy of an original made from cells of the original.
Colonised. Settled in a new country while remaining governed by country of origin.
Colony. Group of living things (people, animals, plants) that live close together.
Commute. To travel to and from daily work.
Conservationist. Person who works towards protection of natural environment.
Continental shelf. Area of shallow sea bordering a continent.
Cultured pearl. A pearl formed around foreign material placed in an oyster.
Customs. Department that collects fees when goods pass from one place to another.
Cyclone. Violent storm caused by air rushing inwards to areas of low pressure.
Deforestation. The removal of forests.
El Niño. A warming of ocean currents which brings drought to eastern Australia and other parts of the world.
Emblem. Object or representation of it symbolising a state, person etc.
Endangered. Reduced in numbers and liable to become extinct unless action is taken.
Engraving. Design cut into hard surfaces.
Escarpment. Long steep edge of plateau.
Estuary. Tidal mouth of large river.
Evaporated. Turned to vapour.
Exotic. Introduced from abroad.
Faunal. Of animals.
Feral. In wild state after escaping from captivity or domestication.
Floral. Of flowers.
Fossicker. One who searches for gold or gems in abandoned mines or workings.
Fossilised. Preserved from a past age.
Glacier-carved. Carved out by moving rivers of ice.
Granite. Hard rock made up of tiny crystals.
Guano. Droppings of seabirds used as plant fertiliser.
Heraldry. Matters dealing with armorial bearings (sets of symbols which identify people or places) on Coats of Arms.
Hydro-electricity. Electricity made by using water-power.
Ice age. A period in Earth's history when ice sheets covered large area of continents.

Indigenous. Originally belonging to a region.
Jousting. Combat between two knights on horseback with lances.
Knots. Units of speed of one international nautical mile per hour (approx. 1.85 km/h).
La Niña. Cooling of ocean currents which brings rain and floods to eastern Australia and other parts of the world.
Larvae. Immature insects.
Lava. Molten rock flowing from volcano.
Lichens. Plants made up of fungi living with algae. They grow on rocks, trees, etc.
Mace. Staff symbolising Speaker's authority in Lower House of Parliament.
Marginal lands. Lands which are difficult to farm and yield little profit.
Mammal. Warm-blooded, fur-bearing animal which feeds its young on milk.
Marooned. Left on shore as punishment.
Marsupial. Mammal whose young ones complete their very early development outside their mother's body.
Megafauna. Large animals which were extinct in Australia by 20 000 years ago.
Mock-Elizabethan. Imitating English style and designs of the late 1500s.
Monolith. Single block of stone.
Monsoons. Wind systems which bring summer rainfall to northern Australia.
Motto. Words accompanying Coat of Arms.
Multicultural. Including many cultures.
Mutineers. People who rebel against authority.
Native. Born in a place.
Navigators. Sailors who plotted the courses of vessels.
Nectar. Sweet fluid produced by flowers.
Oriented. Placed in a particular direction with respect to the points of the compass.
Penal. Concerned with punishment.
Petroglyph. Rock-carving.
Porous. Full of holes.
Predator. Animal which kills and eats other animals.
Prehistoric. From a time before written history.

Quarterings. Four divisions made on a shield on a Coat of Arms by horizontal and vertical lines.
Quartz. Rock formed from silica.
Savanna. Grassland with scattered trees.
Scuba diving. Underwater activity using self-contained breathing apparatus.
Silica. Mineral which occurs as a component of quartz and sandstone.
Silt. Sediment deposited by water.
Smelter. Place where metal is extracted from ore by melting.
Stadium. Enclosed sports ground with seating for spectators.
Stencils. Objects that are painted over then removed to produce patterns.
Suspension bridge. Bridge which hangs on cables passing over towers.
Telegraph. Equipment for sending messages over a distance by electrical connection.
Thermal. Heated.
Threatened. Of a group of animals, liable to become endangered.
Tornado. Violent storm with whirling winds. Moves over narrow track, often with funnel-shaped cloud.
Tributary. River flowing into another river.
Thylacine. Large carnivorous marsupial, Tasmania Tiger, thought to be extinct.
Venom. Poison produced by an animal and introduced into its victim by bite or sting.
Venomous. Full of venom.
Volcano. Mountain having one or more openings through which lava, gases and other materials are expelled from inside the Earth.
World Biosphere Reserve. Place which should be left in its original state to serve as an example of a particular environment, classified by UNESCO.
World Heritage listed. Placed on an international list of places, classified by UNESCO, which are important for cultural, environmental and other values and should be protected.

Acknowledgements

PHOTOGRAPHY: Steve Parish (uncredited photographs). Other illustrations are marked with initials:
BW Belinda Wright
DL Darran Leal
HJB Hans & Judy Beste
JT John Teague, The Photo Library

PES Pat Slater
RS Raoul Slater
TACP Tjapukai Aboriginal Cultural Park
TMAG Tasmanian Museum and Art Gallery
MAPS prepared by MAPgraphics, Brisbane, Qld

The flags and Coats of Arms have been supplied for educational purposes only and are reproduced with kind permission of the Governments of Queensland, New South Wales, the Australian Capital Territory, Victoria, Tasmania, South Australia, Western Australia, and the Northern Territory.

Index to subjects pictured